THE DOWSER'S WORKBOOK

THE
DOWSER'S
WORKBOOK

Understanding and Using the Power of Dowsing

TOM GRAVES

 Sterling Publishing Co., Inc.   New York

1 3 5 7 9 10 8 6 4 2

Published in 1990 by Sterling Publishing Company, Inc.
387 Park Avenue South, New York, N.Y. 10016
Originally published in Great Britain by The Aquarian Press
© 1989 by Tom Graves
Distributed in Canada by Sterling Publishing
% Canadian Manda Group, P.O. Box 920, Station U
Toronto, Ontario, Canada M8Z 5P9
Manufactured in the United States of America
All rights reserved

Sterling ISBN 0-8069-7398-6

Contents

Exercises

1.

Using This Book

Dowsing is a way of using your body's own reflexes to help you interpret the world around you: to find things, to make sense of things, to develop new ways of looking and seeing. And, as the title suggests, this is a *work*book on dowsing: so it's a practical book, with a series of exercises that bring the ideas behind dowsing into a practical, usable context. By using the book in this way, working through each of the exercises in sequence rather than just reading them, you should be able to develop new dowsing skills or improve the skills you already have.

What we learn to do in dowsing is take careful note of certain reflex responses—a small movement of the wrist muscles, for example—and work out what those responses mean according to the context in which those responses occurred. In a way this is little different from what we already do with all our other senses: we use them too to interpret meaning from what we see and hear and sense around us. In dowsing we somehow combine together the information from all those ordinary senses, so that (with practice!) we have just one simple and consistent set of responses to interpret; and we'll generally use some kind of mechanical amplifier, such as a small weight on a string, or a lever such as the traditional dowser's forked twig, to make those responses easier to see and to recognize.

What may seem odd, at first sight, is that there don't seem to be any physical limits to what we can do in dowsing. We can find some things, such as underground water, that we could not possibly see with our unaided senses; and with practice we can also search using information from images—such as a photograph or a map—rather than only from tangible, so-called 'real' objects around us. Although it might disturb scientists, who always have to have explanations as to why things work, it needn't worry us at all: all we need to know, in practice, is how to make sure that we *do* find what we're looking for. Dowsing rarely makes sense in theory, but does work surprisingly well in practice if *you* let it work. We can just get on with whatever we need to do, and let the scientists worry about it afterwards.

But since most people seem to want to know how things work, you will find a small section here on the theory of dowsing, though it's almost at the end of the book. That's because until you have some practical experience—which you'll get by doing the exercises—it will probably be more of a hindrance than a help: so read (and work through) the rest of the book first!

While we don't need to understand how dowsing works, we do need to understand how to use it (which is not the same thing at all). And perhaps the most important thing to understand is that you're not using an 'it' at all: you're using *you*. As I mentioned earlier, what we're really doing in dowsing is learning how to interpret our own natural responses to questions that we put to our environment. Tools such as the old divining rod or the 'pendulum', the weight on a string, do help: but they only help. As in all skills, what really matters in the end is *you*: your knowledge, your awareness. Far more than in most skills, dowsing only works well when you work well: so you can also use your varying results in dowsing as a way of telling you how well you know yourself.

For the same reason, there are no set techniques in dowsing. Everyone is slightly different, so everyone's dowsing techniques will be slightly different. What works best for you now is what works best for *you, now*: not necessarily what worked well for someone else, and, unfortunately, not necessarily what worked well for you a while ago—even as recently as last week or even yesterday. Some dowsers would argue that, once learned, your dowsing skills and techniques need never change. But you change; things change; so your dowsing may well change too. (This is true for any other skill, of course, though it may not be so noticeable). Throughout this book I'll be reminding you of that, to help you learn to notice when and how (and sometimes even why) things change.

To keep track of these changes, use this book as a permanent record. After each exercise you'll find a 'comments' or 'results' box (whichever is appropriate) for you to record what you've found out during the exercise. Do take the time to do this: you'll find it invaluable in the future. For the same reason, leave some space in the box when you write up your notes on an exercise, so as to leave room for future comments.

So, before you read any further, note down what we might call your 'starting position':

Exercise 1: What is dowsing?

What do you know about the subject at the moment? Have you tried doing any dowsing yourself? If not, have you read any other books on it? Summarize your current views below.

Comments:

Akashic record training online

As I've said, you will find that it's useful to have that kind of summary to refer back to later—if only to see how your views change as you gain increasing practical experience. There are no right or wrong answers here: just ones that work well, or not so well, for you, now.

Developing your skill

The idea behind this book is that it can be used as a workbook both to develop your dowsing skills from scratch, or—if you've already had some practical experience—to dip into to improve your skills and to try out new ideas.

There are five parts to the rest of this book:

A beginner's introduction

If you haven't done any dowsing at all before, Chapter 2, *A Practical Introduction*, will get you going, using some 'angle rods', basic dowsing tools that you can make from bits and pieces you're likely to find around the house.

The dowser's toolkit

The next three chapters look in some detail at what dowsers use as tools, and why they're used in particular ways. Chapter 3, *Make Yourself Comfortable*, takes a more detailed look at angle rods, and also at the ways in which our approaches to the skill can make a big difference in the reliability of our results; Chapter 4, *The Pendulum*, will take you through the many variations on what is probably the most popular dowsing instrument; and Chapter 5, *The Dowser's Toolkit*, discusses some of the bewildering variety of instruments that dowsers use as their 'mechanical amplifiers', and will show you the practical reasoning behind the choice of using one dowsing tool in preference to another.

Some applications

In the end, dowsing is only useful if you're going to use it: this section will show you some of the many ways in which you can put your skill to practical use. Chapter 6, *Putting It To Use*, gives practical suggestions on how to build up applications, looking at the basic principle of using dowsing to interpret questions that we present to our environment; Chapter 7, *'Physician, Know Thyself'*, presents some aspects of perhaps the most popular theme in dowsing, its uses in the areas of personal health and fitness; and Chapter 8, *Finding Out*, instead, goes outdoors into the more traditional realm of dowsing, that of looking for things in the outside world.

Making sense

The next two chapters have a change of focus, looking inward but wider at the same time, to put dowsing into a more general context. Chapter 9, *The Greater Toolkit*, gives some practical suggestions to use dowsing—either on its own or in conjunction with other approaches—to look at how we interact with the world and with aspects of ourselves; while Chapter 10, *So How Does It Work?*, shows why attempts to explain the dowsing process create more questions than they answer, and that a more paradoxical approach to theory is perhaps the best way out.

Out in the real world

Finally, Chapter 11, *A Test of Skill*, shows you how to put your new skills and experience to some practical tests—including using map-dowsing and many other techniques to find a real hidden object.

2.

A Practical Introduction

Dowsing is a practical skill, and as such only makes real sense in practice. So, if you've never done any dowsing before, perhaps the first thing we need to do is get you started with some practical dowsing.

All dowsing work consists of identifying when the context of some small muscular twitch can be recognized as usefully meaning something—such as finding the location of an underground pipe or a cable. As with riding a bicycle, we train ourselves to respond in a particular way to various bits of information that we select out from those that happen to be passing by.

On a bicycle, we pay particular attention to data received by our eyes and, especially, from the balance-detectors in the middle-ear, and we compare and merge those together to give instructions to muscles all over the body, to both balance and guide the bicycle. In dowsing we do something similar: but we seem to collect information from *all* of our senses, and direct it to just one set of muscles—usually the wrist muscles—to give the movement that indicates a response.

Because this movement is small and subtle, most dowsers use some kind of instrument, a mechanical amplifier such as a simple lever, to make the movement more obvious. Like the small side-wheels on your first bicycle, they make the learning stage easier; and, as with those side-wheels, they are something that we probably should, in the end, learn to outgrow.

But it's true that it is much easier to use an instrument than to do without: something's *happening*, you can see it and feel it much more easily. So much so that you'll often feel that the dowsing rod is moving of its own accord, as if it has a life of its own. In fact, it hasn't: it will always be your hand moving it. But that *sense* of it 'being alive' is usually a good indicator of when you're allowing things to work, when you're allowing all those internal senses to merge together within you to produce the end results you need.

The other point that we need to recognize even at this stage is that there's no one 'right' way to go about dowsing: there are no fixed rules, only the ways that work for you. But if anything goes, and anything can work, it's difficult to know where to start. It's much easier, at the beginning, to pretend that there *is* just one right way of doing it. Since we do need to start somewhere, we will begin with a set of perhaps rigid-sounding instructions: just note—as in fact you'll find later in the book—that there are many variations, and if you feel uncomfortable with what I suggest here, do try something else until you find an approach that *does* feel right.

Making a basic dowsing tool

The traditional dowsing tool is a V-shaped twig but, as you'll discover later, it's not exactly easy to use. So instead we'll start with a pair of 'angle rods', sometimes known as 'L-rods' from their shape. These can be made from anything that will bend into an 'L' and has a round enough cross-section to turn smoothly in your hand. Fencing wire, welding rod, electrical cable, plastic rod, or even a pair of old knitting needles will do the job, but perhaps the easiest source-material to find is a wire coat-hanger.

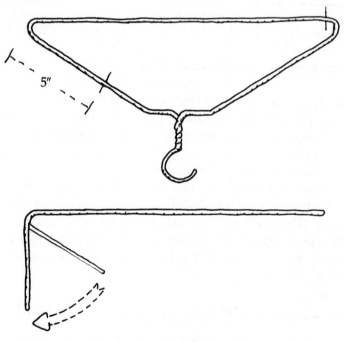

Figure 2.1: Making an L-rod from a coat-hanger

Exercise 2: Make a pair of L-rods

Find a pair of unused wire coat-hangers. Cut the base of one of them at one end, and then just below the hook on the opposite side: the result, a kind of tick-mark shape, should be as shown in Figure 2.1. Bend the short arm back until it forms an approximate right-angle to the long arm, making an L-shape. If the arms are bent, straighten them out, though you don't need to be too precise about it. (If you've used another material, such as fencing wire, make an L-shape of a similar size: for example, around 5 inches for the short arm, 12–18 inches for the long arm). Repeat this to make a second L-rod. That's all there is to it.

Comments:

Having made them, you now need to know how to hold them.

Exercise 3: Holding your L-rods

Hold the short arm of each rod in a loosely clenched fist, and let your arms hang down by your sides. Now bring your lower arms up to the horizontal, with the long part of each rod pointing away from you, as if you're holding a pair of shrivelled cowboy pistols. To be comfortable, keep your arms body-width apart—don't bring them in across your chest. The long arm of each rod should be just below the horizontal (see Figure 2.2). If you hold them tilting down too low, they won't respond easily, and if you hold them too high you'll be spending all your attention just trying to hold them still (like trying to balance on a monocycle!). Make sure that you're holding the rods such that they're able to move freely from side to side.

Comments:

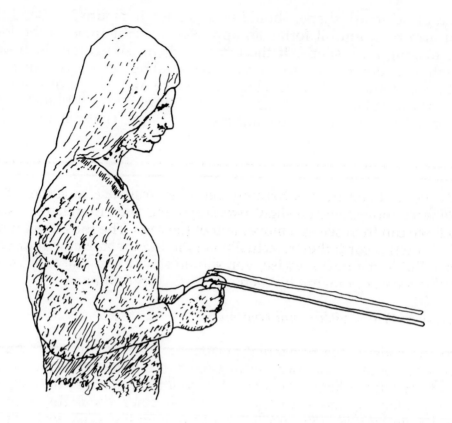

Figure 2.2: Holding L-rods

Held in this position, the rods are in a state of neutral balance, and will thus amplify and make obvious any small movement of your wrists, as the next exercise should show.

Exercise 4: L-rod responses

Still holding the rods in a horizontal position, deliberately rotate your wrists slightly counterclockwise: both rods will turn to the left. Do the same with a clockwise move: both rods will move to the right. Twist both wrists inward: the rods will cross over. Twist both wrists outward: the rods will move apart. Tilt the rods down to about 45°, and repeat the movements: the rods' moves from side to side should be much less. Tilt the rods up about 10° above the horizontal: immediately the rods will tend to fall one way or the other—and stay there—as soon as you move your wrists. (This should always happen this way, for purely mechanical reasons. If this isn't happening, check that you're holding the rods so that they *can* move freely; look at Figure 2.2 if you're in doubt.)

What wrist angle seems most comfortable for you at this stage?

Comments:

_____

What we're doing here is training the reflex response to come out in these wrist movements: a slight twisting of the wrist from side to side, which we can then see as a movement of the rods. The rods don't move of their own accord: they're actually amplifying the movement of your wrists. But in the next exercise, you should slowly find that it *will* seem that the rods are moving by themselves at your command:

Exercise 5: 'Your wish is my command'

Hold the rods in the horizontal position again, but this time change your focus of attention away from your hands and, instead, onto the tips of the rods. Imagine that the rods will both move to the left; ask them politely to move to the left. Don't force them to move by consciously moving your wrists: concentrate on the rods, on watching the rods, on watching them as they move in the direction you ask. Now ask them to return to the centre, pointing away from you to the front. Now to the right; and now ask them to cross over. (You may find this easier if you're moving around a little, as that tends to break any starting friction.) Don't try: just let it happen. Note down your results.

_____

Results:

_____

Although this may sound a little strange, it's actually no different from what we do when riding a bicycle. If you think too much about what your feet are doing or whether you're balancing, you're likely to fall off:

instead, you concentrate on *where you're going*—in other words treat the bicycle as an extension of you rather than as a separate 'thing' which you're trying to control. It does take practice and a certain amount of experience to change the all-too-conscious balancing efforts of your first few bicycle rides, to something where it's so much a part of you that you don't even notice the mechanics of what's involved.

The same is true with these dowsing responses: it does take a little practice before it becomes automatic, before you completely stop thinking about what you're doing, and instead concentrate on where you're going, on what you want to do with the rods.

Exercise 6: Some practice

Go back and do Exercise 5 a few more times. Do you get the sense yet of the rods 'moving of their own accord'? (If you don't, stop trying, and just do it instead: if you try too hard, as with riding a bicycle, it can actually make it harder rather than easier to learn.) Note down some comments on how you feel about it so far.

Comments:

One point you'll notice is that when you let the rods 'move by themselves', they'll move much more smoothly than if you move your hands deliberately. A technique that many dowsers use is to imagine that their rods are some kind of household pet that they're watching and giving instructions and encouragement to, rather than something that they're controlling; you'll probably find it easier to use a similar idea.

One way to illustrate this is to try the next exercise, for which you'll need a partner.

Exercise 7: Following fingers

Stand up and hold the rods as before; have your partner stand facing you, pointing an index finger at the tip of each rod. Now ask the

Figure 2.3: The 'following fingers' exercise

rods politely to follow your partner's fingers as he moves them to and fro (including crossing his hands over so that your rods can cross over, and back again). Let the rods move of their own accord; but make it clear that you *would* like them to follow his fingers. You'll notice that there's a quite definite 'not-trying' state of mind in which the movement clearly happens 'by itself'.

How well did that work out?

Results:

This is, of course, a simple trick to redirect attention and stop the mind getting in the way. But it does work: it does make it easier to use the rods.

Extending your senses

In a way, though, we haven't used the rods at all yet: all we've done is wrist-exercises, getting your reflexes used to the idea of what's expected of them. In each of these exercises you've known exactly what's going on, exactly where the requests for those movements were coming from—namely your own conscious awareness. What we now have to do is to find some responses to things that you *don't* know. And that's where the real magic starts.

Exercise 8: A little magic

Stand up and hold the rods as before, but also making sure that they're balanced so that they're pointing directly in front of you, roughly parallel to each other: what we might call a 'neutral' position. You're now going to walk around with the rods, using them to tell you when some kind of change occurs at the point where you stand at that moment. This time, don't tell the rods to move around: instead, tell them to stay in that parallel, neutral position *unless* your feet pass over some change, some kind of discontinuity—such as if you walk over a water pipe or a power cable—at which point you want them to cross over: 'X marks the spot'. So just wander around the house for a while, and see what you get. Ignore any ideas of cause, or of 'what was it?'—keep your mind open, and just see what you get, see what happens to the rods as you move about.

What kind of responses did you get?

Results:

What you're likely to have had as results to that exercise is a mixture: a few movements you could attribute to plain physical causes such as tripping over the edge of the carpet; a few others where the rods seemed to move of their own accord, perhaps both to one side or the other, perhaps even crossing over; and, of course, a large amount of nothing much at all happening. That's usual at this stage. But now remind yourself of that mental state you reached back in Exercise 5, where you could move the rods around simply by asking them politely to do so. If you didn't ask them to move, they didn't move; if you pushed them to move, it was obvious that you were faking it; but if you asked nicely and just let it happen by itself—'doing no-thing', so to speak— things happened smoothly, cleanly, clearly. Now it's not the action that happened there that we're interested in, but the *state of mind*, of just letting things happen while at the same time setting up some limits or framework for things to happen in. With that in mind, let's go back and do it again.

Exercise 9: A little more magic

Set yourself up to repeat Exercise 8, but this time pay rather more attention to what *you* are doing, what *you* are thinking. Frame clearly in your mind the rules that your rods will follow: that they will remain pointing parallel in front of you unless some kind of change or discontinuity occurs at the point your feet move across, when they will cross over to mark the change. Do set this up, but don't try to make things happen: instead, 'do no-thing' in your mind as you move about. Has there been any difference in the results?

Results:

When you learn to ride a bicycle, there's a knack to the balance which doesn't come together and doesn't come and doesn't come until at some point—usually when you've just stopped trying— it all comes together and you have no real trouble from then on. The same is true of dowsing: there's a real knack to the *mental* balance, the mental juggling-act we've called 'doing no-thing'. Don't worry if it's all a little blurred at the moment: the knack, as with riding a bicycle, *will* come with time and practice.

Go find a pipe

At the beginning of this chapter I said that what we're doing in dowsing is training ourselves to respond in a particular way to various bits of information that we select out from those that happen to be passing by. The key point there is that we *select out* from the mass of information those fragments that are relevant to what we're looking for. If we didn't do this, of course, the dowser's rod would be about as useful as an open-band radio receiver: every channel being played simultaneously in a confusing cacophony of sensory images. It's only when we select out, decide what we're looking for, that we can merge those senses in a useful way into those reflex responses that we use in dowsing.

All our perceptual processes do this kind of separation for us, discriminating between what *we* choose as 'signal' and the rest of the background 'noise': it's sometimes called the 'cocktail-party effect', from the way we can pick out a single conversation in the midst of the babble of a noisy party. To make sense of that kind of noise, we could use a variety of techniques: we might listen to the loudest talker, or point a directional microphone at someone. Or, more often, we can somehow just choose to listen, focus our attention on just one person, almost regardless of how loudly or quietly they're talking, and let our senses merge together to do the rest. And it works.

One of the simplest ways of selecting something to look for in dowsing is exactly the same: just choose what you're going to look for, and let your senses merge to do the rest. So, to complete this instant introduction to practical dowsing, let's choose a simple example, namely looking for a water pipe in or around your house.

Exercise 10: Finding a water pipe

Once again, set yourself up as in Exercise 8, rods held out parallel in front of you, about chest-width apart. This time, rather than looking for *any* change, tell yourself that you're looking for a specific change, a specific thing, namely when you cross over a water pipe. Just tell the rods (remember that trick we met earlier, treating the rods as some kind of household pet) what you want to happen—rather as you just tell yourself that you're listening to *that* person at the cocktail party. If you'd like a little extra encouragement, write it down on a piece of paper—'I'm looking for a water pipe'—and hold it in your hand while you're wandering around with your rods. Start somewhere you can be fairly certain of finding a pipe, such as in the bathroom or kitchen. Go to it! And note down what you find.

Results:

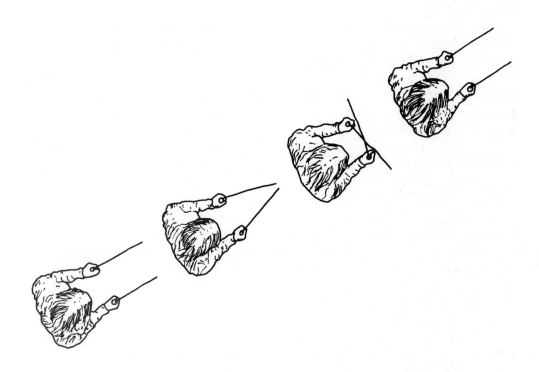

Figure 2.4: 'X marks the spot'—a typical response

With the practice you've had by now, your response as you crossed the pipe should have been something like that shown in Figure 2.4: the rods cross as you walk over the pipe, and then open out parallel again. Don't be surprised, though, if you overshoot the pipe a little, so that you get a slightly different location according to which direction you cross the pipe. (This is because your reflex responses aren't fast enough yet: your body's still a little uncertain of what to do when, rather like that wobbling stage of learning to ride a bicycle.) And don't be too concerned if it didn't work out that way: it doesn't mean that you can't dowse, it just means that you need more practice, of which you'll find plenty as we go through the rest of this Workbook.

So let's move on to look at that practice in rather more detail.

3.

Make Yourself Comfortable

There's no way you can work well in a new skill if you aren't comfortable with it, and dowsing is no exception. And there are two sides to that 'comfortable' feeling: not just being comfortable with the tools you use, but also comfortable in yourself, being confident in what you're doing.

To my mind, most of what we need to learn in dowsing falls into the latter category: it's mainly about interpretation, about what we perceive from the information we receive. That's why dowsing is such an interesting skill, because so much of it depends on you, on who you are—so much so that you can use it as a mirror of how well you understand yourself.

But there is a physical aspect to this, and that's to do with the tools we use to amplify the wrist muscles' dowsing response. Quite small physical changes can make a big difference in how well, and how quickly, angle rods respond to a given wrist movement. So by making pairs of rods in different ways and out of different weights and sizes and types of material, we can explore a variety of subtle if solely mechanical effects on what feels comfortable, on what feels 'right' in a dowsing instrument.

Variations on a theme

Your angle rods are levers which use neutral balance as the mechanical principle to amplify your wrist movements. Everything depends on that balance, and the freedom to move that's implied by a *neutral* balance, neither stable nor unstable.

We looked at some of this in Exercise 4, where we saw the effect that your wrist angle had on how much the rods moved and how easy—or not—it was to keep them stable. The joint-angle of the angle rod itself—between the short and long arms—has a similar effect. To begin with, as in the last chapter, a merely approximate right-angle is quite good enough, but it is worth while experimenting with it to find the angle that's most comfortable for you.

Exercise 11: Adjusting the angle

First make sure that the joint-angle is as close to a right-angle as you can make it, and then hold your rods in your usual position, tilted slightly down from the horizontal. Note carefully how *much* the rods move from side to side as you ask them to move; notice too the feeling in your wrists as they begin to swing. Now take each rod and bend the joint-angle outward a little—no more than 5–10°—and hold them so that the long arms are in the same position as before: you'll notice that they tend to swing back to the forward position. Now try the joint-angle bent inward to an acute angle—again, no more than 5–10°: this time you'll notice that the rods tend to swing outward, and you have to twist your wrists upward more to hold them stable. Bend the joint-angle until you find a position that seems most comfortable.

Comments:

Another very simple change to try is to turn the rods upside-down.

Exercise 12: Upside-down

Stand as before, but this time hold the short arm of each rod the other way up, so that the long arm comes out from *under* your fist instead of above it. Do you notice any difference to the feel of the rods?

Comments:

Some people also like to use handles, so that the rods can turn more easily; others prefer to feel the movement of the shaft of the rod directly against the skin of their fingers. Find out which approach works best for you.

Exercise 13: Using handles

Make a handle for the short arm of each rod from a piece of tubing, or perhaps the shaft of an old ball-point pen or a couple of empty cotton-reels. Note the difference in movement of the rods now that they have a bearing smoother than your hand to turn in. (If you're outside, you may find it useful to rest your thumb on the angle of the rods, to give a little friction to damp out wind-movement.) Do you need to adjust your wrist-angle, or the joint-angle of the rods? Do you feel more or less comfortable using handles with the rods?

_____

Comments:

_____

You'll probably have found that using handles does make a lot of difference: it makes the rods far more mobile but also, in a way, less tangible, less certain; also the wrist-angle and, especially, the joint-angle, become far more critical in their effects on the rods' rate of response. In general, if I'm using a rod made of some relatively lightweight material such as a coat-hanger, I prefer to do without handles; but if I'm using some heavier material such as the 3/16" mild steel rod used in my favourite commercially-made pair (see Fig. 3.1), the handles are almost essential, and do give me a sense of certainty about the response. But that's *my* choice: what works well for you is what works well for *you*, not necessarily what works well for me!

The actual material we use for angle rods can make a lot of difference to how well they work for you, partly for good physical reasons, and partly from a more indefinable sense of what does and does not *feel* right. So it's worth while experimenting by making sets of rods from different materials and in different ways—variations on a theme of angle rods—to see what effects they have in what works well and what doesn't work so well.

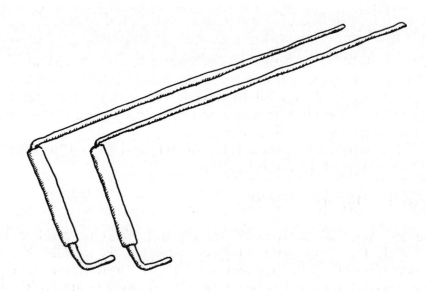

Figure 3.1: Commercial rods with handles

For this group of experiments you'll need a better supply of rod-material than coat-hangers (or you won't have anything left to hang your clothes on!) Two alternatives that should work well and don't cost much are welding or brazing rod, or stiff single-core electrical wire such as earthing cable—both of which you should find at your local builders' supplies store.

Exercise 14: Other way round

The response-rate of the angle rod depends to a large extent on the inertia and the centre of mass of the forward-pointing arm of the rod. To illustrate this, turn the rods the other way round—the short arm pointing forward, the long arm pointing down through your fist—to bring the effective weight down and bring the centre of mass closer to the axis. Try it, and note down the difference in response.

Results:

You'll certainly have noticed a difference there: the response will have been much more twitchy and unstable than with the arms the other, more usual, way round. (If it didn't move at all, you were holding the shaft too tightly, so that the smaller inertia couldn't break the starting friction of your grip. If that's the case, relax a little!) In some circumstances, though, it's useful to have it less stable—you get a faster response—and the shorter length of rod is less likely to get tangled up with the wall as you walk around . . .

Let's continue that theme a little further, and try out the effects of a whole sequence of different lengths.

Exercise 15: Different lengths

Using one material, such as ⅛″ brazing rod, make up a set of pairs of rods, with the long arms ranging between six and 24 inches, at two-inch intervals (in other words 6″, 8″, 10″, and so on—though, as before, these don't need to be absolutely precise). To start with, set the joint-angle of all the rods to the setting that you've previously found to be the most comfortable for you. Now try out each pair, looking for the water-pipe as before, and also trying out some of the other variations, such as adjusting the wrist-angle and joint-angle and using them with or without handles. Which combinations of length and other factors seem to be the most comfortable, or seem to produce the most reliable and consistent results for you?

Results:

Changing the length of the rod changes both the centre of mass of the rod—and thus its response time—and the overall weight. One side-effect of changing the overall weight is that the inertia also changes: if you reduce it too far, the rod becomes more and more susceptible to being pushed around by the wind and similar interferences. One way of moving the centre of mass *without* changing the overall inertia is to mount a small weight, such as a lump of modelling clay, onto the rod, and move that to various positions on the rod. The further away from the axis (your fist, in other words) that you move the weight, the further out goes the centre of mass, and the more-smooth but slower-reacting becomes the rods' response.

Exercise 16: Different balance

Make a couple of small weights—about the size of a grape—from modelling clay, and slide them onto the long arms of your original coat-hanger angle rods. First, move the weights to the middle of the arms, and try out the response. Now move them closer to the axis, and try again. Move them close to the far end of the rods, and note the (considerable) difference in response. Is there any position for the weight which makes the rods' response seem easier than in any of the variations in the previous exercise? Try the weights on other lengths of rod. Do you prefer the rods with or without a weight?

Comments:

The effect is most noticeable when the weight is towards the end of the rod: it tends to emphasize very strongly the swing of the rod. If you like the feel of a weight on the rod, you could also try some other materials such as lead fishing weights. Some dowsers, especially those doing outdoor work, greatly prefer these moveable weights; I don't, as it happens, partly because with them the rods swing around more than I like and partly because they tend to pull my hands down and generally make a long outdoor session that much more tiring. But as usual, it's your choice: see what works best for *you*.

So far we've made all our angle rods out of one kind of metal or another. But there's nothing special about that: we need a material for the rod that's long, thin and as close to circular in cross-section as will turn easily in our hands, and the most common sources of materials that fit that description are metal, such as the ubiquitous wire coat-hanger. We could just as easily make it of some other material, as long as it fulfils our *mechanical* requirements: in fact some dowsers have what you might call a magical objection to using metals at all, saying it frightens the energies away (whatever those might be). Try it out: see if you agree with them. In any case, it's worth while getting into the habit of being inventive, of always being willing to try something new:

Exercise 17: Different materials

This is not so much an exercise as a time to be inventive. You know what you're expecting your angle rods to be able to do, in a mechanical sense at least: now see what else you can make them out of that will still work in the same way. I've used straw, plastic, plant stems, radio aerials (a good one as they fold up inside their handles so that I can put them away in my pocket), candle tapers, pipe-cleaners, knitting needles, and many other things besides. Play with different lengths, different weights, all the other adjustments we've looked at in the previous exercises. See what you can find; see what you can invent for use as a dowsing tool similar to our angle rods.

Comments:

Don't panic if you couldn't think of anything else to use: it really doesn't matter, this is a workbook, not a competition. The point of that exercise was to re-emphasize a theme we'll be returning to throughout this book, namely inventiveness to find what works best for *you*.

Inventiveness has to stop somewhere, and even I was surprised when someone turned up at one of my groups with a beautiful pair of miniature angle rods, to be held between finger and thumb: we'd played with changing the length of the rods, of course, but I hadn't thought of changing the scale of the rods *that* drastically (see Fig. 3.2). He'd designed them for use in map-dowsing, which is something we'll look at later, but they're an interesting variant of angle rods to play with anyway.

Exercise 18: Finger-tips

Make a pair of finger-tip rods, as in Fig. 3.2—probably the simplest

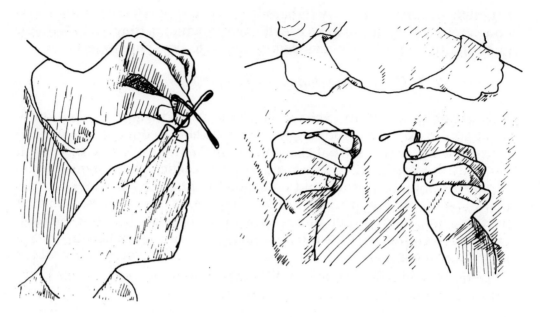

Figure 3.2: Miniature angle rods

materials are medium-gauge fuse wire for the rods and the remains of a pair of old ball-point pens for handles. Hold them between the index finger and thumb of each hand, much as you would hold full-size rods, but probably with your hands much closer together—say, two or three inches apart. Wander around the house with them, looking for water pipes as before. Do you have to move much more slowly? Are there any surprises brought on by this great a difference in scale?

Comments:

Even with rods this small, you'll soon get used to watching the rods out of the corner of your eye, so that you can concern yourself more with where you're going, where you're standing— much as with riding a bicycle. And as with the bicycle, it's at that stage that everything suddenly becomes much easier: you don't have to think about balancing, you just *do* it.

In no time at all you'll find that you can just pick up almost anything that you could use as a pair of angle rods, adjust it to whatever balance feels comfortable for you, and get going. All it takes is practice!

Mind games

The other half of being comfortable in dowsing is being confident with yourself and what you're doing. So, what *are* we doing?

In some ways, to be honest, we don't know. We do know that we're aiming to use those reflex muscle responses to point out when we've found something: but we don't really have a clue how we do it. We just, well, *do* it. Somehow.

This is where most people wander off into theory, and where I will simply sidestep the whole issue by saying that it's entirely coincidence and mostly imaginary.

To make sense of that, we'd better take a brief diversion at this point into some mind games, and then come back to the subject in Chapter 10.

What we're doing is, literally, looking for a co-incidence—with the hyphen emphasized—of where we are and what we're looking for. Just like all our other senses, we're using this 'dowsing sense', this merging of other senses, to pick out a change in the surroundings that's meaningful to *us*, using clues that we choose as being meaningful—such as the muscular twitch that we've trained ourselves to recognize as the dowsing response.

The way that we assign meaning and select 'meaningfulness' is through what we see as the *context* of the event, which we describe through ideas and images—in other words, in what is, literally, an *image-inary* way. We learn to recognize (or, more accurately, choose) that certain things are meaningful, while others aren't: *this* movement of the rods was significant, while *that* movement was simply my being careless and tripping over the edge of the carpet. We interpret the coincidences according to what we see as the context of those coincidences.

This is true for all of our forms of perception: dowsing is no different. I hold in my mind an image of what I'm looking for—'I'm looking for a water-pipe'—and until I've found it, it is, of course, entirely imaginary. What we're learning to do in dowsing is to find a way to bring an imaginary world—what we've decided we're looking for—and the tangible object in the physical world—in this case the water pipe— together, through the overall awareness of our senses. Or, to put it more simply, we're trying to find a way to get us to *know* that we've coincided with the water pipe when we didn't know where it was in the first place.

So we need to know when that event, that co-incidence, has

happened. And to do that we need to have a clear understanding of three simple questions with sometimes not-so-simple answers:

- Where am I looking?
- What am I looking for?
- How am I looking?

All dowsing techniques address these questions in various ways, but let's look at them in more detail as they relate to the use of our angle rods.

Where am I looking?

In order to make sense of a co-incidence—the rods' response— we have to know precisely where it's occurred. At first sight the answer to 'Where am I looking?' seems obvious: I'm looking *here*. But stop and think for a moment: just where *is* 'here'?

Exercise 19: Where is 'here'?

When you're using your angle rods, 'here', the place at which you're looking for a matching response, moves around with you. But where is 'here'? Where exactly is that moving point that the rods' response marks? Is it beneath your feet, your hands, the crossing-point or tips of the rods, or somewhere else entirely? Where do you think—or, better, sense—that 'here' is?

_____

Comments:

_____

We know that 'here' is somewhere down by your feet: but in practice we usually need to be more precise than that. We need to know exactly where that pipe is; we need to know the exact place on the ground meant by that co-incidence of the crossing of your angle rods. Since that point isn't obvious, we *choose* one.

This perhaps sounds a little strange, but it really is no different from the way we *choose* to listen to one person rather than another at some noisy party. Our perceptual systems can—and do—select out the timing of information, giving us warnings about relevant co-incidences: here we're just making use of that inherent ability of ours in a slightly different way. We *choose* where 'here' is.

The hard part, then, is making sure that the rods know, so to speak, of where your choice of 'here' happens to be. So, just tell them: it's as simple as that. As with riding a bicycle, your senses will do the rest, once they know what you want. But if you can't make up your mind, there's no way that your dowsing can be accurate. So choose.

With angle rods, the best choice is often 'the leading edge of the leading foot'.

Exercise 20: Marking 'here'

Stand holding your rods in their usual forward-pointing position, and look down at your feet. Imagine that just above the ground, and just touching the fronts of your shoes, is a fine black line, at right angles to the direction you'd walk in. This line, which marks 'here', can extend outward sideways to infinity, or shrink to an infinitesimal dot. As you move your first foot forward, it moves too, as if pushed forward by your foot. When you place that foot down, and bring the other past it as you walk, this imaginary line moves forward with the leading edge of the leading foot. And you're asking the rods to cross over when what you're looking for (such as the water pipe) coincides with the place marked precisely by this moving line of 'here'. As the rods respond, stop, then move back: the rods should open out again. Standing on one foot, slowly bring the other foot forward, pushing 'here' across the spot again with more precision; again, the rods should cross as your foot moves over the place, and re-open as it moves past. With a little practice, you should be able to tell exactly where the pipe starts and ends.

Results:

By choosing to mark 'here' in different ways, you can resolve some practical problems that might otherwise be awkward. For example, it's difficult to track a pipe close to a wall, because the rods tend to get tangled up with the wall as you walk closer to it. So one solution is to change the way you mark 'here', simply by walking *backwards*.

Exercise 21: Backs to the wall

Start by holding the rods in the usual way, and frame in your mind that you're looking once more for that water pipe. But instead of imagining that fine line of 'here' at your toes, draw it at your heels. Now look for the pipe in the usual way: but search *backwards*, walking backwards, with 'here' being moved back by the leading edge of the leading heel. In this way you're able to back right up to a wall without the rods hitting it, but you still get responses in the usual way. How do you get on with this perhaps rather strange change to the rules you've worked with so far?

_____

Comments:

_____

You can mark 'here' in any way you like, as long as you can make clear to yourself where 'here' is. If you're using a pendulum for dowsing (as in the next chapter) rather than angle rods, you can use a hand or a finger to point out 'here', or point in a particular direction, with the line of 'here' stretching outward from you to infinity. Or you can be more imaginative, and say that 'here' is the place *represented* by some point on a photograph or a map—hence map-dowsing, of which more later.

It's up to you. It's *all* up to you. That's the great strength of dowsing; but it's also the reason why it can sometimes take a great deal of practice and discipline to get it to work well.

What am I looking for?

The rods' reaction at some place shows that we've found a co-incidence with something there: but it's difficult to know what they mean unless we know that we're looking for something. We have to tune the radio, so to speak; we have to be selective, we have to *choose*.

So, almost before we do anything else, we have to decide what we're looking for: otherwise (to use our anthropomorphic analogy) the rods won't know what to respond to, to mark the co-incidence that we'd like. One of the real disciplines in dowsing is in learning how to be clear, precise and specific about what it is that you're looking for.

One way to do this is simply to hold the object in your mind: in other words, say to yourself 'I'm looking for . . .' (whatever it is—a water pipe, in our previous examples). Frame it in your mind: imagine it, *image* it.

Exercise 22: Image-ination

What does that water-pipe look like? What is it made of? If you could touch it now, what would it feel like? Use your other senses: smell, taste. Listen to the sound of the water moving through; feel the coldness and wetness of the water in the pipe. Build an image of the pipe, and everything it implies, in your mind. *That* is what you're looking for. With this image held in mind, try looking for the pipe once more. Does it make any difference to the results?

Comments:

Another common method is to carry a sample of pipe material with you, to use as a tangible reminder of what it is that you're looking for. One commercially-made dowsing kit, designed for use by surveyors, actually came complete with a set of samples of piping materials wrapped around one of the rod-handles—see Fig. 3.3. (For historical reasons, American dowsers tend to refer to this kind of sample as a 'witness'.) Or you could write it down on a piece of paper as a kind of verbal sample—'I'm looking for a water pipe that's like *this*'—or perhaps draw it: anything, as long as it's a useful prompt to make it clear to your rods (in other words you) what you want their response to coincide with.

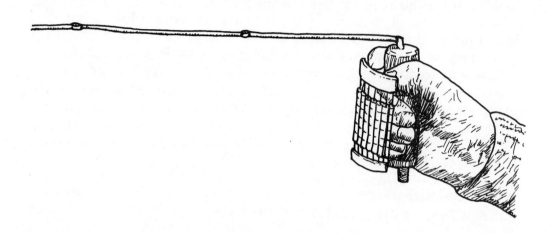

Figure 3.3: 'Revealer' rods with set of samples

Exercise 23: Using samples

Many people find that using a tangible sample—something you can actually touch and hold—makes their dowsing that much easier, helping them to focus more clearly on what they're looking for. Try out for yourself various types of sample: an actual piece of pipe, a written message, a little sketch, even a photograph of piping from some catalogue. What difference—if any—does this make to the reliability of your results?

Results:

You can, of course, find things other than water pipes with your angle rods. In principle, you could find *anything*, since all you're doing is using the rods to indicate the co-incidence between where you are and what you're looking for. In practice, of course, we tend to look for more tangible objects: cables, keys, cashew nuts, or whatever. All we do is change the rules: tell the rods that we're looking for *this*, rather than the pipe as before. Try it:

Exercise 24: You choose

Using the same techniques as before, look for something other than a pipe: a coloured thread placed under the carpet, or a nut hidden underneath one of several cups. Choose what to look for, then 'image-ine' it in your mind, or hold a sample or 'witness' of it, or whatever other way you choose. Remember, look for it without trying: it's an exercise, not a school test. Keep in mind this idea of 'doing no-thing': just let yourself find it. And note down what happens.

Results:

Whenever you're using the rods, there's always a little 'noise' mixed up with the signal: the rods drifting this way and that at times, for no apparent reason. At this stage you'll probably be just beginning to recognize when there's a real 'signal' response from the rods: there's a quite different feel to it, a sense of '*this* one'. But while most of the other twitches and wanderings may well be meaningless, don't be too quick to dismiss them all as 'noise': sometimes they're trying to tell you something.

The same is true at that noisy party, of course: sometimes you'll hear interesting snatches of conversation that drift out of the background babble—or important messages such as 'Food's ready!'. The dowsing equivalent would be the rods giving you further information about what you're looking at, such as a joint or branch in the pipe, or the direction the pipe's going in; or else telling you that you're walking over something that's not specifically what you're looking for, but may be relevant and that you ought to know about, such as an electrical cable that needs repair.

One of the important tricks in dowsing is to leave some kind of space in the rules that you're using, so as to allow these 'not-in-the-mainstream' messages to come through—rather as you'd keep half an ear open, so to speak, for other information at the party. As at the party, the best indicator is always that clear 'feel' when something is meaningful—it 'stands out from the crowd', we would say; but one way to help it is to build other types of responses, in addition to 'X marks the spot', into the rules that you set up for your rods to follow.

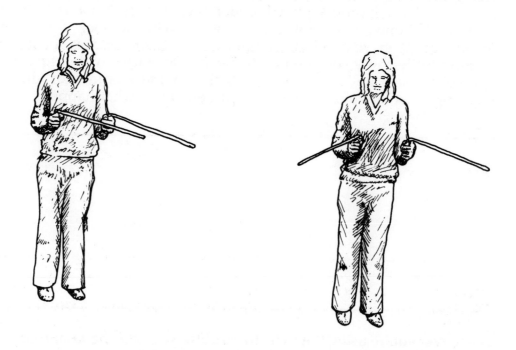

Figure 3.4: Some more responses: direction and 'something else'

A good example of one of these extra rules, or extra response types, is what we might call 'they went thataway', for which the rods both move parallel to point out a different direction (see Fig. 3.4). You could also set up that the rods move in a similar way to point out a shape or an edge—particularly useful if you're trying to find buried walls at an archaeological site, for example. And another move is what I call the 'anti-cross', in which both rods swing *outward* instead of inward—I set this up in my list of rules to tell me that there's something else important here, even if I've not specifically been looking for it (somewhat the equivalent of hearing 'Food's ready!' during your conversation at the party).

Exercise 25: Asking for directions

Find the water-pipe as before, with the previous rules of 'X marks the spot' and telling the rods what you're looking for in the way you've found works best for you—sample, written message, an image held in your mind, or whatever. Once you've found the pipe, walk back a couple of feet; let your arms hang down for a moment. Now change the rules: instead of crossing over, ask the rods to *point out the direction of flow* (it may be a good idea to turn the water on for a moment to make this easier). Bring the rods up again, and walk forward over the pipe with this request in mind. What response do you get?

Results:

Practice with this for a while, switching between the two sets of rules: 'I'm looking for the pipe (or whatever)' and 'I'm looking for the *direction* of the pipe'.

Having found the direction, it would now be useful to track along the pipe instead of marking it with a series of passes of 'X marks the spot'. We can do this by asking the rods to *continue* to point out the direction that we should move in so that we can walk directly along the course of the pipe.

Exercise 26: Just keep on trackin'

Find the pipe as before; then re-cross it with that change of rules so that you can find the direction to follow it (either upstream or downstream, whichever's more practical). Still with the idea of 'direction' in mind, adjust the rules slightly: you now want the rods to point towards the line of the pipe, swinging back across the pipe if you move off the line, and pointing out any changes of direction wherever there's a bend in the pipe. You may find it helpful if you encourage the rods to hold a slight 'squint' whenever you're on the pipe, and to open out to the standard parallel 'neutral' position if you're no longer above it—in other words a kind of mixture of 'direction' and 'X marks the spot'. Try it: see what you get.

Results:

Don't be too concerned if what you've mapped out is best described as a drunkard's walk, rather than what was supposed to be the straight line of the pipe. How well could you travel in a straight line when you first learnt to ride a bicycle? Not exactly a straight path then, was it? The same is true here: until you've had a lot more practice, you will often tend to 'hunt' or overshoot the line, over-correcting each time you cross the pipe—hence the wandering line that you've marked out. The *overall* course probably will be correct, even now, when you come to check it out. Once again, all you need is practice!

Along with that you'll also need practice at that balance of looking for something specific, some specific co-incidence, whilst at the same time keeping yourself open and aware for other possibilities, other information.

Exercise 27: Pardon the interruption

Repeat some of the previous exercises in this chapter; but as you do so, take particular note of any places where your rods consistently move in a 'something else' response, or some other way than those we've specifically set up for that exercise. If so, can you work out what the rods are responding to? Does any particular image or suggestion come to mind? This is something we'll be returning to later, but note down your feelings or sense about this at this stage.

Comments:

What we're doing in dowsing, in effect, is building layer upon layer of rules for the rods to follow, to tell them exactly what co-incidence to respond to. Layer upon layer of rules within rules, sub-clauses, ifs, buts and perhaps, all building up as precise a description as we can of what exactly it is that we're looking for and in what context (or contexts) we're looking for it. In a way, we're *programming* the response of the rods, rather like programming a computer.

However, the computer here is not some external machine, but our own overall awareness, sensing for some specific co-incidence. The computer program has its input and output; the input here is that merging of all our senses into what seems at times to be a separate sense, and the output is directed into one place, the reflex muscle responses that we see and feel in the movement of the angle rods. The catch, as in computing, is 'garbage in, garbage out': if you don't take enough care over the instructions you set up for that 'bio-computer', the results will, all too often, turn out to be nonsense, rubbish, garbage. So it's important to consider not just *what* you're doing, but also *how* you're doing it, what your mental 'set' or state of mind is while you're working.

Which brings us back to the third of those three questions that we need to ask.

How am I looking?

The way in which you approach any skill is important; but in dowsing it's absolutely critical. Approach your work with the wrong state of mind, and you'll usually find yourself getting nowhere slowly. Your mind-set matters. A lot.

As with riding a bicycle, there's a delicate balance to be learnt: a balance of mind rather than body. Assume you can't do it and, yes, you're right, you can't do it. Alternatively, assume that you know exactly how to do it, you know everything there is to know about it, and, strangely enough, you'll probably find that you can't do it. What actually does work is even stranger: try extremely hard for a while, and then quite deliberately give up. Just let it happen, without trying, and it works, as if by itself, with you doing 'no-thing' to make it do so.

Do nothing, and nothing happens; do something, trying to make it happen, and and once again nothing happens; instead, you have to reach that delicate balance of 'doing no-thing'.

It's perhaps easiest to understand that balance by exaggerating what *not* to do.

Exercise 28: Why bother?

Set yourself up to look for that pipe again. Proceed exactly as before:

but this time just introduce a few doubts in your mind. Dowsing doesn't work . . . it's all coincidence anyway . . . the few apparent results I've had so far were just chance and that's why it hasn't worked since . . . in any case I'm never going to be able to get good at it, so why bother . . . and so on. Does this 'I can't do it' mind-set make any difference to your results, compared to previous exercises?

Results:

Here we've been exaggerating, of course, but those nibbling little doubts and under-confidence with which most people start are likely to have much the same effect. The trouble is that those inner doubts are subtle, so their effects are subtle too. Learn to watch your responses closely, and you'll see how your dowsing can become a useful mirror of your current state of mind.

The same is true of over-confidence, in that it can wreck your results just as effectively as doubt.

Exercise 29: The world's greatest dowser

Let's go looking for the pipe again. With a new, breezy, hyper-confident mind-set: 'I'll do it: you won't need to check my results, because I'm always right. I'm perfect, the best, I'm the world's greatest dowser'. What difference does this make?

Results:

Well, it may have given your confidence—and your results—a boost for a while, but the most common ending of that is the phrase 'Pride comes before a fall'. A big one. A long, long drop. If you ever reach a point where you're certain you know it all, that's when you're likely to be just that little bit over-confident—with disastrous results. Every skill is a learning experience, for a lifetime: you never can get quite perfect. And if you spend much energy on protecting your ego from the inevitable bruises, you'll never get much done. So again, your dowsing can become a useful mirror of that aspect of your current state of mind: by watching your results, you can watch yourself at the same time.

Over-confidence and under-confidence are variations on a much more wide-ranging theme of *assumptions*. We assume things to be such-and-such a way; since these then form part of our mind-set while we're working, they're included in that list of rules that we set up for the rods to respond to in marking the coincidence we've said is going to be meaningful. So the rods, obliging as ever, will respond exactly according to that list of instructions—leaving you to disentangle the confusion of whether they responded to a real object like a pipe, or an imaginary 'object' like 'I can't do this'. If your instructions to the rods—your instructions to you, that combining of your senses—are riddled with assumptions, it's not going to be too likely that your results will be of much use.

This applies not only to attitudes like over-confidence, but also to assumptions about repeatability and the like. Let's take a typical example.

Exercise 30: 'I got it here last time . . .'

You'll need to borrow a friend to help you with this one. Get them to hide something, such as a length of string under a carpet, or a marble under one of a set of cups. First, try to find the object in the usual way (it doesn't matter if you don't find it, though: that isn't the purpose of this exercise). Your helper then, without you seeing, either moves the object, or doesn't: and try once more to find it. Watch particularly for assumptions like 'I got it there last time...': if you allow that kind of idea to take hold, what happens to your results?

Comments:

It's up to you—your choice. You can spend all of your time looking for imaginary objects: your rods will quite happily find them for you in some imaginary world, but not, unfortunately, in this so-called 'objective' world that we happen to share with everyone else. Or you can pay attention to what assumptions you're placing on the way that you work: in which case you might well get some useful results. (With practice, of course!)

There are occasions, though, where you can put the blocking effect of assumptions to practical use, by deliberately ignoring some information that would otherwise get in the way—rather like shutting out the gabbling of some loud-mouthed oaf at the party so that you can listen to the quiet-voiced woman next to you. In other words, we *declare* that something is 'noise', even if it was useful information a few moments ago. Just ignore it, tell yourself that it isn't there any more— rather as you would wish was the case with the loud-mouthed oaf!

One example would be when trying to find something with water in it, *other* than the water pipe.

Exercise 31: Ignorance is bliss

Set yourself up to find water as usual, but this time looking for lines of underground water in general, rather than specifically for the water pipe. You should find the pipe as before, but also (in most cases) some new 'image-inary' lines. Now repeat the exercise, but this time tell yourself 'I know that the pipe's there, I don't need to know about it, what *else* is there to find?' Do the rods still respond to the pipe when you include this in the mind-set? Do those other 'water-lines' become easier to sense? Is there any difference in *feel* between these lines and the pipe, beyond the similarity of the rods' response to them?

Comments:

Properly used, this kind of 'selective ignoring' can be an immensely powerful tool. We have in fact used it already, back in Exercise 25, to get the rods to show us direction rather than position; and again in

Exercise 26, where we followed the course of that one pipe and ignored any others that we might have crossed.

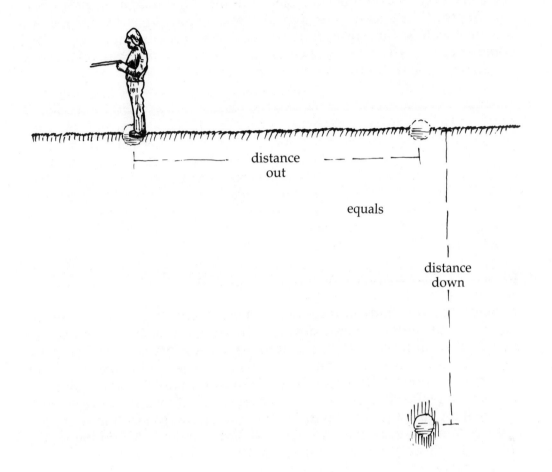

Figure 3.5: Finding depth with the 'Bishop's Rule'

We can use a similar process to find the *depth* of the pipe, with a technique known in dowsing circles as the 'Bishop's Rule' for at least a couple of centuries (see Fig. 3.5). We mark a point directly above the pipe; then when we get another response from the rod, the distance back to where we started will be the same as the depth of the pipe at our starting point—in other words, 'distance out equals distance down'.

Exercise 32: The 'Bishop's Rule'

First find the pipe and mark its position, in the usual way. Now change the rules: ignore the pipe itself, and ask to find the *depth* of the pipe at that point. To do so, imagine that, instead of walking outward, away from the pipe, you're walking *down* from the surface toward the pipe: the rods' response will occur when you meet the image of the pipe at that depth. (Move slowly—a typical pipe will only be a few inches or a few feet below the surface. If it isn't, you have something wrong somewhere . . .) Try this in several directions from the same place, and at different places along the pipe, and see what results you get.

Results:

In all of this, do be inventive, and do remember to check things out for yourself. For example, some dowsers find that the Bishop's Rule works in a rather different way: 'distance out' may be half or twice the distance down, or some other factor. And that won't be very helpful if you've presumed that someone else's assumptions about experience (which in reality is all a 'rule' is) must apply to you: you may find yourself digging a great deal further than you thought to find that pipe!

And remember to maintain that delicate mental balancing act of 'doing no-thing': asking politely for things to happen, and letting things happen the way they want to in return. It *is* a subtle balance, and it does take practice: but if you've been doing the exercises rather than just reading them, you'll be well on the way to reaching that balance by now.

4.

The Pendulum

For a number of good, practical reasons, the pendulum is without question the most versatile and most popular of all dowsing instruments. It is also, to my mind, the one that's most often misunderstood and misused. It all looks so simple: but it's easy to use badly, and not at all so easy to use well.

Although in principle it's an even simpler tool than our angle rods (because in its basic form it's just a small weight on a length of string), its movements can be deceptively subtle—and subtly deceptive. To use it reliably, we need to develop some real skills in interpretation: not just of the pendulum's rapid responses but also of our state of mind and all the other conditions that go into the questions we set it.

We've done much of that work already in the last chapter, in a way in which we could see what was going on, and learn in practical experience. That's why we started with angle rods, rather than jumping in at the 'deep end' with the pendulum. It may be a simpler instrument *mechanically* than our angle rods, but it can be—and is—used with a far wider variety of approaches and contexts. You do need a proper understanding of the principles you're putting to use, otherwise that variety of choice can be bewildering—with sometimes embarrassing effects on your results.

Precisely *because* of its versatility, we need to use the step-by-step approach perhaps more with the pendulum than with any other dowsing instrument. Once again, though, there are no set rules: it's up to you. I'll be describing what I know has worked for me and for others: both the practical approaches and the principles behind them. But the key to understanding dowsing will always be you and your awareness and inventiveness, learning what works best for *you*. Keep that in mind, then, as you move through the exercises in this chapter!

Make it yourself

You can buy purpose-built pendulums in many places—alternative bookstores, mail-order houses and the like—but in some ways it's preferable to make your own. The commercial ones may be better balanced, and have all sorts of interesting features such as hollow spaces for 'samples': yet they can't quite match the *feel* of something that's personal to you and you alone.

Mechanically speaking, a dowsing pendulum is just a weight held in neutral balance, either downward on a piece of string or, sometimes, horizontally at the end of a spring—a form known to American dowsers as a 'bobber'.

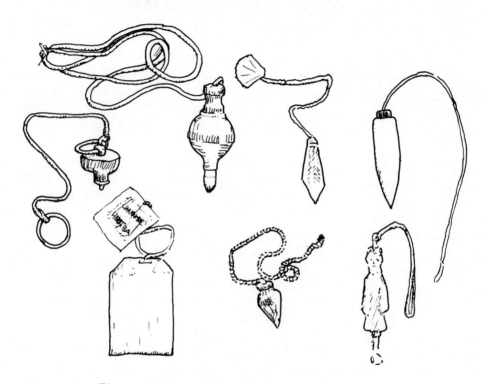

Figure 4.1: An assortment of dowsing pendulums

There are some practical limitations, but, to a large extent, anything goes (see Fig. 4.1). A builder's old-fashioned brass plumb-bob is almost ideal; many people may only use a favourite crystal tied to a length of thread; but I've found that a damp used tea-bag works surprisingly well—just the right weight and balance! Small trinkets are popular, too, precisely because they have a personal feel to them. One of my students used a tiny plastic white elephant as a pendulum; and another, a somewhat eccentric sculptor, even used a large pottery gnome on a heavy length of rope for a while—but it was reshaped in a somewhat unfortunate disagreement with a wall, after which he was forced to revert to a rather more conventional dowsing tool!

For the next few exercises you'll need a basic pendulum that's well-balanced and whose length can be adjusted easily. Look at some of the examples in Fig. 4.1 and see if you already have something suitable in your house—something like the builder's plumb-bob, for example, rather than a bunch of keys or a trinket. If not, you can make one.

Exercise 33: *Making a basic pendulum*

Three suggestions. Go to a fishing supplies shop and buy a lead 'sinker' fishing-weight weighing between half an ounce and two ounces, and some lightweight nylon line; tie about 12 inches of the line to the top of the weight. Or find a spare cotton-reel, and squeeze some modelling clay down through the spindle-hole to give it some extra weight; then push a medium-sized needle into the centre of the clay, and tie about 12 inches of thread through the eye of the needle. Or else find a used AA-size battery, wrap it with rubber bands, and pierce a hole for the thread through the bands at the top. Whichever way you choose—ready-made or home-made—hold the thread or line between finger and thumb, about two inches from the top of the weight. Swing the bob gently backwards and forwards, slowly increasing the length of the thread to about six or seven inches. Are there any lengths at which the bob moves more smoothly than otherwise; a length at which it seems to be 'swinging itself'?

Comments:

When the pendulum swings, it's because your hand is moving it—or starting it moving, at any rate. As with angle rods, there's no reason to invent another cause: the pendulum moves because your hand moves.

For good mechanical reasons, the length of the thread and the way you hold it do affect that movement, though. The muscles in your hand will have a number of natural 'resonant' rates that vary somewhat according to factors such as mechanical load: so if the swing-time of the pendulum matches one of those rates, the pendulum will respond much more easily, whilst other lengths will tend to counter that natural muscular response, actually dampening the pendulum's movement. So let's try that part of the exercise again.

Exercise 34: A natural balance

Hold the thread between finger and thumb, and swing the pendulum bob gently backwards and forwards. Once it's started moving, don't bother pushing it, just watch it. Can you feel it working with the natural movement of your hand, or do you find yourself restarting the swing all the time? Adjust the length of the thread several times until you find one at which the pendulum needs no effort from you to keep going once you've started.

Comments:

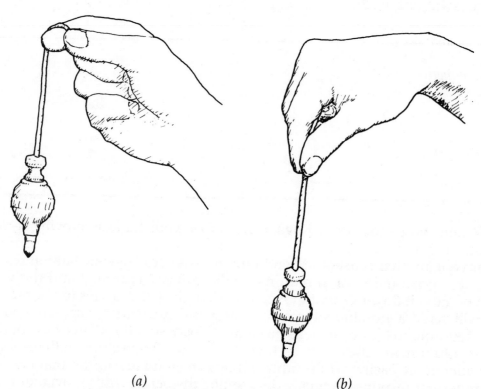

(a)   (b)

Figure 4.2: Two ways to hold the pendulum thread

The way in which you hold the thread matters too. Many people start by holding it draped over the first joint of the index finger, holding the thread still with the thumb (see Fig. 4.2a). The trouble with this is that the effective length of the thread keeps changing, and sometimes the finger itself is in the way: a better grip is the one I call 'holding a distasteful worm' (Fig. 4.2b), where the thread is held between the downward-pointing finger and thumb.

Another advantage of this second grip is that you should have a better feel of what the pendulum is doing, without needing to look at it, because the thread is held by one of the most sensitive parts of the body—the fingertips. I prefer this grip, but you might prefer the other, so try it out for yourself.

Exercise 35: Keeping a grip on yourself

Hold the pendulum with each of the two grips shown in Figure 4.2—note that the best length for the thread, as we experimented in the last exercise, may be slightly different for each. Which grip do you prefer? Which one seems to give a better sense of control? Try other ways of holding the pendulum; see what you can invent.

Comments:

The pendulum bob is just a weight on a thread, swinging back and forth in response to your initial and subsequent pushes one way or the other. Like the angle rods, it's in what is called 'neutral balance', which means that it can move about but won't fall over; and so, like the angle rods, we can *ask* it to move in various directions.

Exercise 36: A few moves

Hold the pendulum in whatever way you've found comfortable, and swing it gently back and forth so that it feels like it's moving by itself. Now ask it politely (as we did with the angle rods) to change the movement to a gyration, swinging round in a clockwise motion. And ask it to return to the to-and-fro oscillation. Now ask for a counterclockwise movement, and then back to the neutral oscillation. Try a side-to-side movement; a diagonal move. Do all of these movements by *asking* the bob to move, image-ining it moving in that direction rather than pushing it to do so.

Comments:

As with the angle rods, we can assign meanings to these various movements: meanings such as positive and negative, Yes and No, direction, and the like, all according to the context. As usual, we choose which movement means what, although there's a certain amount of natural choice as to which movements work best for what meaning: the back-and-forth movement for neutral, and the gyrations for Yes or No, for example.

But before we look into that, there's a slight matter of inertia. The pendulum's much easier to use—and certainly faster-responding—if it's *moving*. Some writers on dowsing suggest that you should hold the pendulum still, and wait for a movement—any movement—to indicate a response. The result can mean a lot of waiting, but some dowsers do prefer this:

Exercise 37: *A matter of inertia*

Hold the pendulum in the usual way, and let it swing gently back and forth in a 'dynamic neutral' movement. Now ask it to change the swing to a gyration (clockwise or counter-clockwise, it doesn't matter which), and note how long it takes for the movement to change to a clear gyration. Stop the pendulum: ask it politely to come to a complete halt, a 'static neutral'. As before, ask the pendulum to start a specific type of movement (again, you choose). How long does it take to get to a *distinct* type of movement? How does this compare with the time it took to get started from the dynamic-neutral movement?

Comments:

Inertia also accounts for one reason why the shape of the weight you use as a pendulum bob can be important. Ideally, the weight needs to be a compact shape, with the centre of mass quite close to the point where you attach the thread. To see what *doesn't* work, try the following experiment:

Exercise 38: Another matter of inertia

Find a pencil and the usual length of thread, and tie the thread to the top of the pencil. Go outdoors, or stand somewhere where there's a light breeze. Start your pencil pendulum swinging; set it moving in various other movements. How easily can you distinguish those movements from the natural wobbling of the pencil on the thread? Now stop, and re-tie the thread in the *middle* of the pencil. Once again, set this pendulum swinging; set it moving in various other movements such as gyration. Can you distinguish any of those movements from the natural antics of the delicately-balanced pencil?

Comments:

A long, thin, horizontal weight is about the worst possible design for a pendulum: it will always be highly unstable, much as a pair of angle rods tilted upwards are never going to be easy to use. You can use whatever you like for the pendulum weight: but do make sure that you take mechanical considerations like inertia into account!

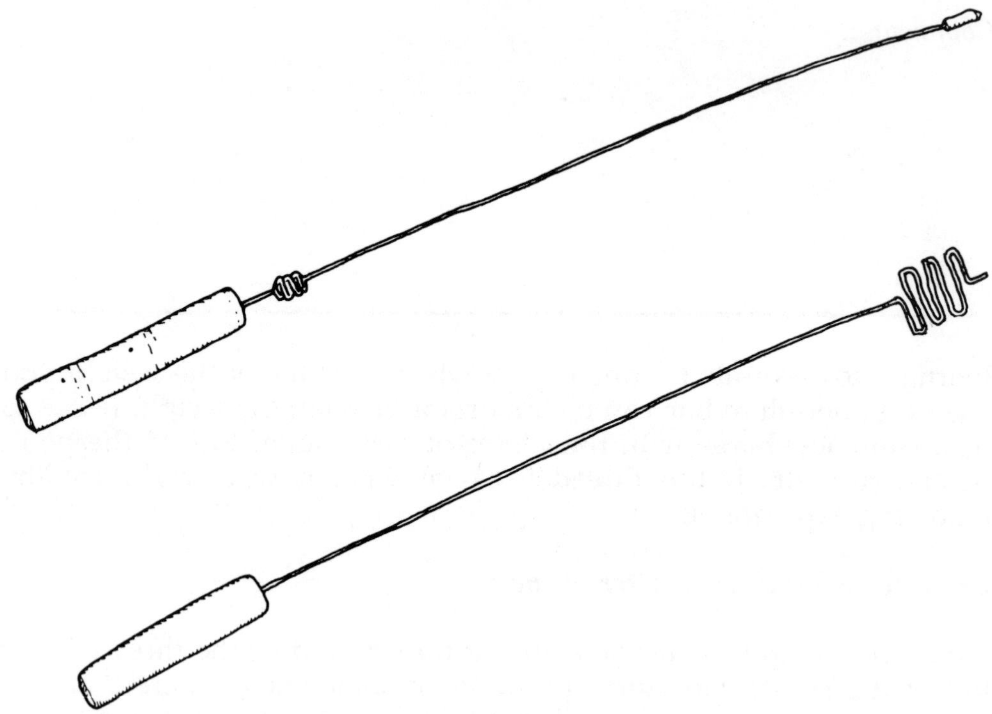

Figure 4.3: Two ready-made bobbers

So far we've only used a vertical pendulum: a string with a weight hanging from it. An alternative approach is to move everything into the horizontal plane, with a weight—or even no weight—attached to a long, thin springy rod, typically metal or plastic. One shown in Fig. 4.3 (known as a Pasquini Amplifying Pendulum) has a spring at one end and a small plastic weight at the other; on the other bobber, the folded section that looks like the business end of a fly-swatter is simply to increase the effective weight at that end; but sometimes people do without any extra weight at all.

Exercise 39: Making and using a bobber

To make a simple bobber, push a thin (1/16″) and long (about 2 feet) piece of welding or brazing rod through a cork. Hold it out horizontally, with the cork in your hand; bob the end of the rod up and down slightly, as if it were a pendulum that's been moved to the horizontal plane. The natural movements for a bobber are slightly different: it's not quite so keen to move in a gyration, and a popular dynamic-neutral is to have it move in a diagonal path, lower-left to upper-right. Note too that changing the length of the rod has a much more noticeable effect than on a pendulum, because of the springiness of the rod: which length works best for you?

Comments:

Some of my students found that a spring-loaded bobber such as the Pasquini design was the easiest instrument with which to start dowsing. But it shares one of the disadvantages of angle rods, in that it does tend to get tangled up with walls as you walk around!

In any case, now that you have a pendulum or bobber that you can use, we can add it to our toolkit.

Exercise 40: Putting a pendulum to use

Go back to the area you searched for the pipe with your angle rods. Set up your pendulum in its neutral mode, moving or static. Now frame in your mind, as with the angle rods, what it is that you're after: you're looking for that pipe. And you want the pendulum to respond, to the co-incidence of you and the pipe, by moving to some other mode than the current 'neutral': any movement from a static-neutral, or else a gyration, say, from the dynamic-neutral I recommended. Note that you may have to move more slowly at first than you've become used to with angle rods. How easy is it to find the pipe?

Results:

You can use a pendulum in exactly the same way as angle rods, using different movements to point out a direction or to track along the pipe. You can use the *angle* of swing of the pendulum, moving away from the forward-and-back dynamic-neutral, to point out a direction, for example. Or you can use the Bishop's Rule to work out the depth of the pipe, as before: it's a different instrument with a slightly different set of responses, but the principles are exactly the same as those with which we've already experimented.

You can also use a pendulum in a quite different way: and that's where things get interesting.

Yes and No

The simplest way to use a pendulum is to get it to answer questions. One type of response means Yes, and another means No: one question leads to another, to another, to another, until you find the answers that you need.

You can in principle do this with any dowsing instrument, but in practice it's easiest with the pendulum. Its response time is so much shorter, for the usual mechanical reasons; and, unlike angle rods, for example, there is no starting friction to overcome before it can respond to the question you've given it. Angle rods work best when you're moving around, while a pendulum is often best if you're sitting still, letting it do your moving for you.

In order to make use of this, though, you first need to identify the pendulum responses that to you will mean Yes and No.

Exercise 41: Finding Yes and No

Write on two pieces of paper the words 'Yes' and 'No'. Hold your pendulum in your preferred neutral state (my recommendation, if you're in doubt, is to swing it gently backward and forward) above the 'Yes' piece of paper. Concentrate on the idea of 'Yes', affirmative, anything that goes with 'Yes'; build that as an image. Ask the pendulum to show you what response means Yes, what response it would give in relation to that image. Try it two or three times. Once you're fairly certain of what that response looks like and, perhaps more important, feels like, do the equivalent exercise with the 'No' piece of paper, using the idea of negation. What responses do you get?

Results:

It is important to make sure that you do have quite different responses for Neutral, Yes and No. Sometimes people will suggest that the pendulum should just stand still, and *any* response will then be a Yes: but that does cause real difficulty. There's a lot of difference between a non-committal Neutral and a definite No!

It's also useful to develop the *feel* of that Yes or No response: you can work a great deal faster, for example, if you don't have to wait for the full-blown pendulum response but can know which answer it's going to be, from the kind of move that the pendulum's *beginning* to make. And there's a lot you can learn by watching the degree to which it responds, or the speed with which it responds: sometimes (if the Yes response is a gyration, for example) it will give a violent swing that's unquestionably a Yes, while at others the response is a rather half-hearted elliptical wobble that's best described as a 'sort-of Yes'.

If you don't yet have a consistent set of responses, it may be that your pendulum (which in this sense is, as always, you) hasn't yet got the message about what you want it to do. So tell it. Assuming that we start with a dynamic Neutral—the pendulum swinging backwards and forwards—the easiest way to distinguish Yes and No is to have the pendulum move into different gyrations, such as clockwise for Yes, counter-clockwise for No. (For some peculiar reason for which, as usual, I have no explanation, the most common default responses seem to be different for left or right hand, and for men and women.) If you haven't already found a consistent Yes/No/Neutral set of responses, try Exercise 42.

Exercise 42: You set the rules

Swing the pendulum in Neutral above the 'Yes' piece of paper. Ask the pendulum to show you which gyration—clockwise or counter-clockwise—is Yes. Now do the same with the 'No' piece of paper. If you get the same result—both clockwise, for example—complain gently to the pendulum, explain that you need *different* responses for each, and go back and do it again. While you're at it, try the exercise holding the pendulum in the other hand. Are the results any different, or any more consistent?

Comments:

It may take you a little time, but you *will* get there. You will get a consistent distinction between Yes and No. Even if the pendulum never quite gets to be consistent, you'll eventually notice a distinctive difference in *feel* between Yes and No, which the pendulum does amplify but is quite noticeable on its own. But that, as they say, is a matter of practice!

Yes and No are only one of many types of *polarity*: others are positive/negative, masculine/feminine, and so on. We can train the pendulum to recognize these for us in much the same way.

Exercise 43: Polarities

Using the idea of a polarity of 'masculine'/'feminine' in an energy rather than gender sense, hold the pendulum over your left knee, then your right knee. Try the same over a friend's hands or feet, and over a number of different objects: test the polarity rather in the sense that some languages such as French will class objects as masculine or feminine. Note down your results. For the second part of the exercise, try a different polarity, that of positive or negative charge, over the terminals of a battery: train yourself to recognize them, and then try it 'sight unseen', with a friend hiding the battery in, for example, a 35mm film canister. How accurately can you find which battery terminal is upward in the canister?

Results:

One interesting point to watch is that if you get it more wrong than right—such as consistently the wrong battery terminal—you're actually doing well. All that's wrong is that you're not *recognizing* the right answer: you haven't trained your pendulum well enough, so that it tends to think you mean Yes when you mean No, and vice versa. If necessary, go back to Exercise 41 to help clarify this before going any further, otherwise little of what follows is likely to make much sense.

Once you do have a clear distinction between a Yes and No response on your pendulum, you can then ask it questions: any questions to which a Yes or No response would be meaningful. By 'asking a question', we mean that we frame the question as a kind of context, and see what response of the pendulum happens at the same time—in other words we're looking for the co-incidence of what we're looking for (the question) and where we 'are' (the pendulum's response).

Exercise 44: Question and answer

Ask a friend to hide your keys somewhere in the house. And now, using a stream of questions, use your pendulum's Yes/No responses to find out where the keys have been hidden. Remember, the question must be unambiguous, and must be phrased such that a simple answer of Yes or No will make sense. So are the keys upstairs? If so, are they in the bedroom? Are they in the bedroom closet? And so on, until you find them. How easy do you find it to make sense of the answers you receive from the pendulum?

Comments:

The trap here is that the questions *must* be unambiguous, and they *must* be phrased such that Yes or No makes sense. You can't ask 'Is it upstairs or downstairs?': that question can't be answered meaningfully by either Yes or No—unless the answer is neither, which is probably even more confusing. Or, to take another example . . .

Exercise 45: What do I do now?

Hold the pendulum in Neutral, then ask it 'What do I do now?'. What response do you get?

Results:

It's not exactly helpful if the pendulum answers Yes to that one. With Yes or No as the only permissible answers, there's no way it can make sense—a classic problem of 'garbage in, garbage out', to use computer jargon. What we have to do instead is 'un-ask' the question: move back a step so that we rephrase the question in a different way, such that Yes or No *can* make sense. And it's useful to set things up so that the pendulum can tell us when we need to un-ask a stupid question, through what I call the 'idiot' response.

Exercise 46: The importance of the idiot

Hold the pendulum in neutral and ask the pendulum for its 'idiot' response, a response that means 'un-ask the question'—that the question being asked cannot be answered either by Yes or No. Make it clear that this Idiot response must be recognizably different from either Yes, No or Neutral. To help it, test it with a question such as 'What do I do now?' What response do you get?

Comments:

My own Idiot response is a side-to-side motion, at right-angles to the Neutral, so *my* basic set of pendulum responses (for my right hand) are as in Figure 4.4. There are others, of course, but these are probably all you need to use the pendulum successfully with this kind of question-and-answer system.

The hardest part of this style of dowsing is finding not the answers, but the questions. Each answer leads you to new questions, but the pendulum can't often help you in choosing *what* questions to ask. It's up to you: *you* are the one who's fishing for facts, questing for questions. And not just questions, but ways of phrasing those questions such that Yes or No (or Idiot) can make sense. It's all too easy to slip up with a double question such as 'Do I go left or right?', or a double-negative like 'Was the last answer wrong?'—in which No could be either No-means-false (in other words *not* wrong) or No-means-negative (in other words it *was* wrong).

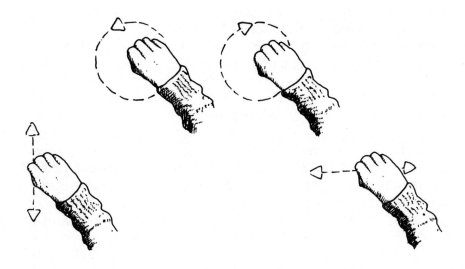

Figure 4.4: A typical set of pendulum responses

Many people use check-lists, charts or diagrams: they do help, but they'll never have *all* the questions ready-made for you. It does take a fair amount of practice to describe what you mean in a clear, precise way: you'll need to end up with much the same sort of devious layer-beneath-layer thinking as the good computer programmer, trying to trap every possible loophole in the chain of questions and answers. For example, let's look back at the battery experiment we did in Exercise 43.

Exercise 47: Avoiding ambiguity

Hold the pendulum over the battery inside that film canister, and ask 'Which way up is negative?' (You'll probably get an Idiot response if you try it.) What's wrong with that question? Work out a way of phrasing that test such that it's unambiguous and bypasses the other traps mentioned above.

Comments:

To be truly precise, you could well have ended up with some legalistic tangle such as 'Is the positive terminal of the battery facing upwards at this (upper) end of the film canister?' You can get away with less, of course, but you do have to be very clear to yourself about what you mean!

Styles of use

There are, of course, other ways to use a pendulum. As we saw earlier, you can use some kind of sample or 'witness' to remind you of what you're looking for, much as we did with the angle rods. Some of the commercially-produced pendulums have a hollow space inside to hold a small sample, but it's just as easy to hold it in your hand or your mind.

Exercise 48: Using samples with a pendulum

Fill three glasses with water, and dissolve a small amount of sugar in one of them. (You could ask a friend to do this for you, or to shuffle the glasses around.) Now use your pendulum to find which glass contains the sugar solution. To help you focus, hold a physical sample of sugar, either in the pendulum itself, or in your hand, perhaps wrapped in a small twist of paper. Swing your pendulum in Neutral over each glass in turn, watching for a coincident response of the pendulum. Now try again holding just a conceptual sample—the word 'sugar' written on a piece of paper—and then once more just saying to yourself 'Does this glass contain the sugar solution?' You can test your results by taking a sip from the glass you choose. How do the results of the three different approaches—physical, conceptual, image-inary—compare?

Results:

We can also point out a direction or follow the line of a pipe, for example. One method is for you to turn round, pointing outward, using the pendulum to say when you're pointing the right way; whilst in another method we can ask the pendulum itself to point out the right direction.

Figure 4.5: Pointing out a direction with the pendulum

Exercise 49: Pointing with a pendulum

You now want to use your pendulum to find True North. First, hold your pendulum in your preferred hand, and point outward with your other arm (see Figure 4.5). You're looking for True North: you want the pendulum to respond when you're pointing in the direction of True North. Turn round slowly with this idea, this image in mind: see what responses you get.

_____

Results:

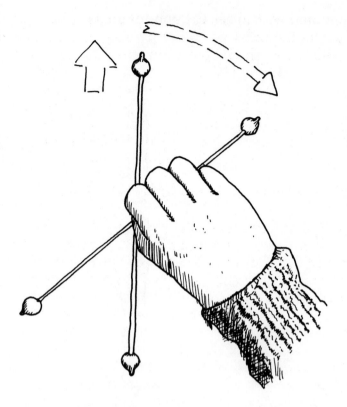

Figure 4.6: Directional response with the pendulum's axis

Now try another approach to the same problem:

Exercise 50: Getting the pendulum to point

Swing the pendulum in Neutral, and ask it to move its *axis of swing* to point towards True North (see Figure 4.6). Try this twice, setting the initial Neutral axis of swing in two different directions. How do the results compare with those from the previous exercise? Which method do you prefer?

Results:

Some of the older pendulum-dowsing techniques assumed that there was some kind of natural resonance between the pendulum and what you were looking for: linking the 'vibrations' together, so to speak. One example is Tom Lethbridge's 'long pendulum' system, which uses the concept that when the *length* of the pendulum thread matches the vibrations from your chosen object, the pendulum will naturally move from Neutral to a response such as gyration. You tune the pendulum to different target objects by adjusting its length; then by adjusting the length you can select what you're looking for.

Exercise 51: Experimenting with the long pendulum

Make a 'long pendulum' with your usual bob attached to a thread at least four feet long, wound round a small windlass such as a pencil. Set the thread length as short as practicable, and hold the pendulum in neutral over some object such as a gold ring; slowly increase the length of the thread until the pendulum starts to move off Neutral into a gyration. (Note that this may happen at more than one length.) Measure the thread length, from fingertips to bob top, at this point. Repeat with a number of different objects. Having done so, set the length of the pendulum thread to one of your recorded values, and try looking for that object with this length or 'rate' as in our previous exercises. Is this more or less reliable than the previous 'short pendulum' technique? Are they any obvious disadvantages of the long pendulum?

_____

Comments:

_____

One of the earliest systems for pendulum dowsing used this concept of resonance in a slightly different way. Holding the pendulum over an object, the dowsers found that it would gyrate a few times—a count they called the 'serial number' of the object—and then stop, or at least drop back to oscillation for a few swings. This pattern would then repeat, sometimes with variations—two gyrations, four swings, three gyrations, four swings, and so on—with the whole sequence being called the 'series' of the object.

Some dowsers maintain that these 'resonant properties' of objects are constant and objective, but that's not what my students found: the rates, series and serial numbers, and the like were different from one person to another, though often constant for each person. That's something you'll have to find out for yourself, by watching, observing, recording.

Exercise 52: A habit of observation

Take some time to look around you with your pendulum. Try out various ideas such as resonance and number with different objects. Change the properties of each object you test in sequence—a brass ring, a copper ring, silver, gold, glass, plastic—in such a way that as far as possible you're only changing one property at a time. Use your inventiveness and your awareness to create new techniques, and develop the careful observation of the scientist: record your results with care, always watching as much for what *isn't* there as for what is there. Note down some comments now; return to it at a later date, and compare notes!

Comments:

Often in dowsing we need to know not just where something is, or its qualities, but quantities as well: how far, how much, how often, and so on. There's not much point in drilling a well if there's only a little trickle of water at the end of it; and in any case you'll need to know how far to drill.

We have met up with one technique already, namely the Bishop's Rule—'distance out equals distance down'—for finding depth. And it's easy to see that we can use a sequence of Yes/No questions—'Is it more than five feet down?', '. . . ten feet?',' . . . twenty feet?'—for the same purpose. We use Yes/No questions for any quantities, of course: 'Is the water-flow more than 100 gallons per hour?' or 'One lump of sugar?', for example.

Alternatively, harking back to the series/serial-number techniques, we can ask the pendulum to gyrate the right number of times to match the quantity we're looking for, and then simply count turns of the pendulum—although, as Tom Lethbridge once found, this can be tedious if the quantity you're after is in the thousands! To avoid that, you can, as usual, change the rules: one turn of the pendulum for a count of ten, or a hundred, or perhaps a tenth of the quantity you're measuring.

Exercise 53: Numbers—how much, how far?

Using the comments above as a guide, use your pendulum to find the depth of the pipe at various points, and also to estimate the volume of water flowing in that pipe. Compare the results of various techniques. Which ones do you prefer? Which ones seem most reliable?

Comments:

In Chapter 3 we looked in some detail at how we can *choose* how we mark 'here', the place we're looking at. Using angle rods, we could choose the leading edge of the leading foot, or the back of the heel, or some other place. With the pendulum, you'll usually have one hand free, so we can use an arm to point out a direction (as in Exercise 49). Or we can use a finger or some small pointer—a pencil, for example—to mark 'here' with far more precision than we could do using 'the leading edge of the leading foot' as our marker.

The real advantage of this precision is that it allows you to work on a small enough scale to search on maps or photographs or diagrams. You work in exactly the same way as before, except that, to use the telephone company's slogan, you're letting your fingers do the walking, moving around in an *image* of the place. You're searching for a co-incidence between what you're looking for and the place *represented* on the map—not on the map itself.

The advantages of map dowsing are obvious: you can walk through walls, and cover vast areas of ground, all without leaving your armchair. The disadvantage is not so obvious at first, and has caused

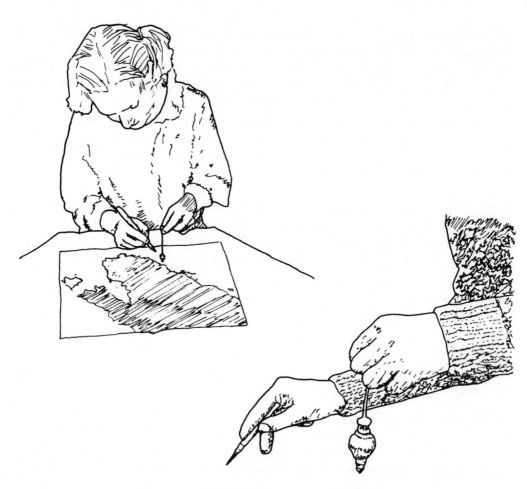

Figure 4.7: Map dowsing—using a pointer

many dowsers considerable embarrassment and grief: you have to be *very* skilled in allowing your senses to reach out to the place which that image-inary point on the map represents, and not be distracted or confused by wishful thinking and all the other dangers of dealing with imaginary worlds.

There is, of course, no way that map-dowsing can make sense in physical terms, but that needn't bother us too much: we can leave that until Chapter 10. For now, all we need to know is that it *can* work—if you let it. 'Here' is the place *represented* by where you're pointing to on the map: apart from that, we use exactly the same dowsing techniques as before. You will need practice to get it reliable, so try it for yourself.

Exercise 54: Map dowsing—imaginary worlds

Find an architect's plan of your house, or draw a diagram of it yourself. Once again, look for the water pipe; but remember to clear your mind of previous experiments and approach it as if you've never looked for the pipe before. Hold a pointer in one hand, your pendulum in the other: move the pointer across the diagram, reminding yourself that you want the pendulum to respond when the pointer is over the site of the pipe as *represented* on the diagram. Use the change-of-axis directional response (see Exercise 50) to plot out the course of the pipe, moving the pointer around as if you were walking around in the places that the map represents. Now compare your results with your previous experiments in the physical world: how well do they match up?

Results:

It is important to check your map dowsing results against physical reality, to give you feedback on the reliability of your work, and also to make sure that you don't drift off into some imaginary dreamland. Map dowsing is so easy, waving your pendulum around in the comfort of your own home, that it's anything *but* easy to keep a firm grip on reality. Dowsing is only useful if we put it to *practical* use: and to my mind searching for the lost treasure of the Incas, or chasing past lives in Atlantis, don't quite fall into that category!

The same applies to dowsing at a different time. Dowsing always works with 'here' and 'now', a position in space and time, which, by default, is the same as the conventional reality's physical definition of here and now. But in map dowsing we redefine 'here' as some image-inary place, and in time dowsing we redefine 'now' in the same way. There's nothing to stop us doing so, other than our doubts; but we have to use the same amount of care as with map dowsing, to make sure that we can get the image-inary world implied by some other time to merge with the here and now of physical reality.

To make things worse, our concept of time is beset by some intractable paradoxes, which creates several nasty traps for dowsing in time—something else we'll look at in Chapter 10. For the moment, all we need to know is that we can look to the relatively near past (a few days or decades, depending on what we're looking at) and an even closer future: beyond that, it becomes less and less reliable. But for practice, let's look at weather patterns, past, present and future.

Exercise 55: Weather patterns—dowsing in time

Several national newspapers list the previous day's weather at a number of cities around the world. Using your pendulum, make up a log of weather predictions at a few of those cities. Standardize your questions: sunshine hours, rainfall, percentage cloud cover, temperature at a specific time of day ('the time the newspaper uses for its temperature figure'). Each day, before reading the newspaper, go through your list three times: 'now' in time is yesterday, then today, then tomorrow. Compare your results against the previous day's entry in your log; then check your 'yesterday' results against the newspaper's data. Do this for at least a week. How precise can you get it?

Results:

By now you should be able to get results more accurate than guesswork, but don't expect wonders: you're not likely to get perfect predictions at this early stage of the learning curve. Accept that you're learning: as with any skill, you'll get better with time and practice. You also need to keep checking your results against physical reality, to give you the feedback you need in order to improve: without it, your results will remain forever imaginary. Dowsing is a *practical* art, a *practical* skill: keep it that way!

5.

The Dowser's Toolkit

Angle rods and pendulums are only two of the tools in the dowser's toolkit: we have plenty more to choose from if we need. In past times people used anything from a strip of willow to a bucket handle—even a twisted length of German sausage—but always to the same end: to amplify the muscular response to that combining of all the senses, marking that co-incidence of what we're looking for and where we are.

For dowsers of the past, their divining rods quite literally grew on trees. When you wanted one, you went to a suitable bush and cut a V-shaped fork out of it. Only certain trees and bushes would do: hazel, cherry, dogwood, hawthorn, and some others. In tune with the times, it was thought that these types of wood had special magical properties. In tune with *these* times, we might well still agree about the magic, but note also that they share particular physical properties: springy, resilient, symmetrical branching—just what we need for a mechanical amplifier of that muscular twitch we call the dowsing response.

The idea of the V-rod was that it was somehow 'pulled down' to point to underground water—an illustration in one eighteenth-century religious tract even shows the divining rod being pulled downward by some little demon. We can see it in a different light: the rod is a spring-loaded lever, so that when your wrists move a little, the rod moves a lot. It's up to you which belief-system you choose, of course: what matters is how well you can put the tools and that belief system to use.

Using the V-rod

For dowsers, the traditional V-shaped twig or 'spring rod' is in some ways like the doctor's stethoscope: people don't quite believe you if you don't know how to use one. But like the stethoscope it's not as easy to use as it looks, which is why we've not tried to use it until now.

To work, the rod has to be held in a state of unstable tension: but just the right amount of instability. The difficulty is in learning how to balance the thing. You have to be able to hold the rod under considerable tension whilst still being completely relaxed in mind and body. Too much tension and you're fighting to keep control, whilst too little tension leaves it about as responsive as a limp banana.

A few people do have a strong natural response to underground water, and have no difficulty at all in using even the great inch-thick lumps of wood that some dowsers used in the past as their spring rods. But for the rest of us it's a delicate if unsubtle balance that can be very elusive—hence the traditional idea that only a few 'gifted' people could ever be dowsers. More recent instrument designs such as the pendulum and angle rods have proved that notion to be false, but the myth still lingers on. Do try the spring rod, but don't be surprised if you can't get it to work well for you: many professional dowsers can't use it either.

Figure 5.1: An assortment of V-rods

You can buy ready-made spring rods from some specialist suppliers or the national dowsing societies, but if you make your own you'll have a better idea of what works and what doesn't. You can either cut one out of a suitable tree, or make it up out of two strips of some suitably springy material (see Fig. 5.1).

Exercise 56: First find your tree . . .

Look at the trees and bushes around you when you're walking outside. To make a spring rod, you need to find a tree whose branches fork in a 'Y' rather than the more common one-side-then-the-other-side, so that when you tense it it bends symmetrically. The wood needs to be springy and resilient—a firm spring that you can push against and will survive being bent many times. It needs to be clear of other forks for at least 10–12" (ignore leaves and small thorns, as you can easily strip those off). The thickness can be anything from perhaps ⅛" to ½", but you have to be able to bend it when cut into a V-shape, so that it fits comfortably in your hand, pointing away from you, and can turn as required. When you've found something suitable, ask permission of the tree and, if necessary, the owner, and cut out a usable fork (see Fig. 5.2). What kind of trees or bushes will do the job?

Comments:

If you can't find a tree, you can probably find two strips of some springy material to bind together. One traditional material was whalebone, which is (for very good reasons) all but unobtainable; you could use the kind of flat spring that's now replaced it in corsetry, or spring steel, or certain types of plastic that have a good spring and resilience.

Exercise 57: Spring things

Look around for suitable materials for a spring rod. What you're after is some material that you can bend round in a curve at least 90° that you have to apply some effort to bend that far and that snaps back sharply

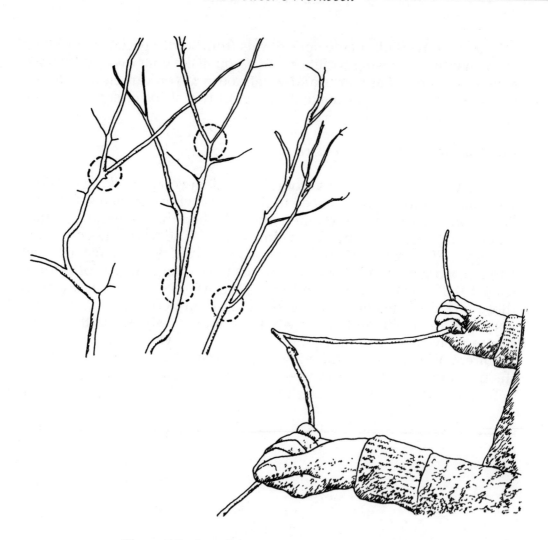

Figure 5.2: A traditional V-rod: cutting and holding

to its original shape when you let go. It can be a rod, such as a nylon knitting needle, or flat, like a springy metal ruler; the plastic bristles from a yard brush will work well, too. You need two, anywhere between six and 18 inches long: note how different lengths of the same material give a quite different effective springiness. What materials can you find? When you've found them, bind them together at one end to make a 'V' shape.

Comments:

One way or another, you've now made your V-rod. To use it, you now twist it into an unstable spring, so that a small movement of your wrists results in a large movement of the tip of the rod.

Figure 5.3: Two ways to hold a V-rod

Exercise 58: Holding a V-rod

If you have a V-rod made of a tree-fork or some round material such as nylon rod, close your fists round the arm of each rod; if your V-rod is made of some kind of flat material, hold each strip between two fingers and thumb. Now open your arms out, palms upward, to tense the 'V' into a spring (see Fig. 5.3). Twist your wrists outward slightly: the rod tip should move upwards sharply, pulled by the spring. If it doesn't do this, increase the twist on the arms of the rod to increase the tension; if you're fighting it to stay stable (the equivalent of tilting your angle rods up too far), slacken off slightly. Remember that the idea is to use the rod to amplify your wrist movements, but to do it so well that you don't notice your wrists moving at all: when you get this right, it will seem like the rod has come alive in your hands. Experiment with different tensions, different grips (palms up and palms down, hands close together or far apart), and with rods made of different materials.

Results:

_____

If nothing much is happening, you haven't applied enough tension: the grip is quite critical, and with some materials you'll need to apply a surprising amount of force. It's not an easy balance, but practise at it for a while.

To use it, we now need to apply the other half of the balance: at the same time as holding the rod in tension, you need to be relaxed in yourself. Set up the same state of mind as when you were working with angle rods or the pendulum, and go looking for that pipe again.

Exercise 59: Find that pipe (V-rod)

Remind yourself that you're looking for that pipe. Tense up the V-rod, and ask it politely to keep its tip horizontal until where you are—that moving point we've called 'here'—coincides with what you're looking for. At that point you want the tip to rise or dip sharply, to mark the place, the co-incidence. If nothing happens, check how you're holding the rod, and try again. But watch out—once you've sorted out that balance of tension correctly, the sharpness of the movement could take you by surprise! How does this compare with using angle rods or the pendulum?

_____

Results:

_____

The V-rod isn't an easy tool to master: but once you have done so, it's a very satisyfing instrument to use. The response is so strong, in a way that really does feel like the rod is coming alive in your hands, that there's no doubt: what you're looking for is *there*.

One minor point is that, certainly in the early stages, it's even more sluggish than angle rods unless you're moving around. Some dowsers do use it to point out direction, turning round on the spot until the rod springs up to mark a line, but it's not easy. And because of the tension it can be a tiring instrument to use, too. But do experiment with it.

Exercise 60: Adapting techniques to the V-rod

Experiment for a while with different sizes of rod, and apply some of the ideas that we've looked at in previous chapters. Look at ways of adapting the different sample techniques: physical, conceptual, mental. Use depth techniques such as the Bishop's Rule; see if you can use an up or down movement of the rod as Yes or No—and if so, what response would Idiot be? Find *your* way of putting the V-rod to use.

Comments:

One limitation of the V-rod that you'll have noticed is that in itself it doesn't have a good directional response: it can't swing to one side or the other to point out a direction, as both angle rods and pendulum can. But with one ingeniously simple modification, adding an extra arm to make what we call a W-rod, we can make it much better in this respect. The disadvantage is that in this form it isn't as good as a V-rod for marking a single point (a classic example of a trade-off!)

Using the W-rod

Unlike a V-rod, the W-rod doesn't grow on trees: you'll have to make this one!

Exercise 61: Making and holding a W-rod

Bind another arm of the same length and material to the holding-end of one arm of a V-rod, making a shape like a squashed 'X' with a linking bar across the top. Grasp opposite arms of the new rod, and unfold them into a tense curve like a 'W' or 'M' (see Fig. 5.4)—in effect two V-rods sharing a common arm at the front. Hold it with the same kind of tension as you used for the V-rod. Its movement is much the same if you twist both wrists inward or outward at the same time; what happens if you move the wrists differently?

Comments:

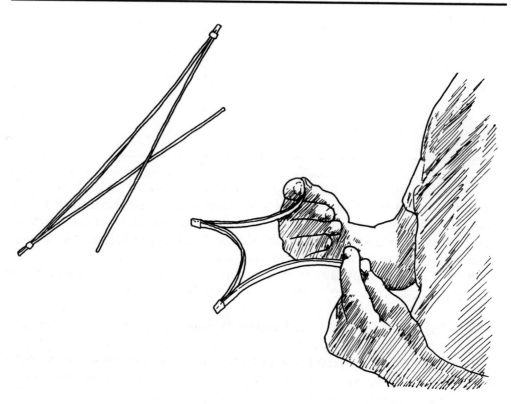

Figure 5.4: A W-rod at rest . . . and ready for use

As you'll have noticed if you did that exercise, the rod dips to one side or the other if you move your wrists in any kind of asymmetry—so much so that the rod can end up twisting around itself if you're not careful. But this directional dip can be very useful if we're trying to track along something linear such as a pipe.

Exercise 62: Following a pipe (W-rod)

Find the pipe in the usual way, asking the rod to dip to the downflow side as you cross it. Turn to face that direction, and relax for a moment. Now hold the rod again, and make it clear to yourself that you now want to follow along the pipe, using the rod to tell you when you're no longer directly above it. Tell the rod that you want it to stay horizontal while you're above the pipe, and to dip to whichever side you're drifting off, so that you can correct it and move back over the pipe. Doing this, the feel is often like 'riding' the pipe as if it's a linear hump in the ground, like a low wall on which you're balancing as you walk. What do you sense as you follow the pipe with the W-rod?

Results:

As with the V-rod, we can adapt some of our other techniques for use with the W-rod. Because it has more range of movement than the V-rod's simple up-and-down, we can, for example, adapt the pendulum's Yes/No system to the W-rod.

Exercise 63: Yes, No and Polarities (W-rod)

Write the words Yes and No on two pieces of paper. Ask the W-rod to give a different response for each, then move the rod over each piece of paper to see what you get as Yes and No. Try out some of the other polarity experiments from Chapter 3: for example, set up the battery experiment again, with an AA-size battery inside a film canister. Can you set up the W-rod to rise on one side for the positive pole of the battery, and to fall for the negative pole? What movement could you set up as an Idiot response?

Figure 5.5: 'Riding' a pipe with the W-rod

Results:

It will, as usual, take a little practice to get this to work well, and it's true that the W-rod is more cumbersome than a pendulum. But do try it for a while, if only as a comparison to the relative simplicity of a pendulum.

The W-rod is perhaps best suited for finding shapes of objects: as we saw in Exercise 62, it 'rolls' over edges, dipping and rising. And another instrument that was purpose-built for that job is Verne Cameron's 'Aurameter'.

Using the Aurameter

Cameron's Aurameter is a peculiar hybrid of a dowsing instrument: half-way between an angle rod and a bobber, with a few other ideas mixed in between (see Fig. 5.6). The single arm pointing outward has a coiled spring at one end and a weight on the other, like a bobber; but it's hinged in the handle so that it can swing from side to side like an angle rod, with a light spring to centre it. Unlike angle rods, the handle is held horizontally; the angle of the bobber, and for that matter the weight, can be adjusted to change its mechanical sensitivity.

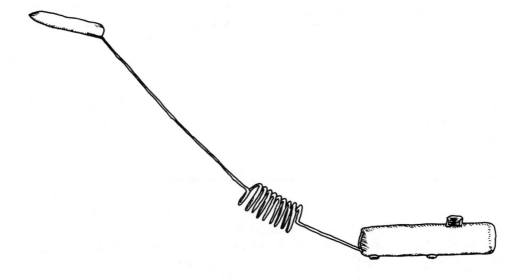

Figure 5.6: The Aurameter

Because of all these features, it's not a simple instrument to make yourself—though it's probably worth while if you want to experiment with it, as commercially-made versions are relatively expensive. The following exercises can be done in a similar way with a bobber or a single angle rod, though the Aurameter does have a clarity of feel to it that makes it easier to use than the simpler instruments.

As its name implies, the Aurameter was designed to measure auras. Exactly what auras are, or are supposed to be, is not something that we'll go into here: suffice it to say that it's useful to imagine that a field of some kind exists around the human body (or other bodies), and that we can measure the shape and other properties of this field by bringing a dowsing instrument up to or through its edge.

Exercise 64: First find your aura . . .

You'll need a friend to help you with this exercise. Imagine that around your friend is some kind of aura or field of energy, extending some distance outward. There are several layers to this aura, but the one we want to look at is closer in to the body, no more than about two feet outward. So hold your Aurameter (or equivalent) at that distance, and bring it inward slowly towards your friend's body, asking it to react when it meets up with the edge of this aura. It should respond by twisting away, as though brushing against some kind of cobweb-delicate surface. Try this at different heights around the body, from feet to above the head; once you've done this, try it around the cat, around machines, around plants. What shapes do you plot out?

Results:

As a comparison, you should also try these experiments with a pendulum, bringing your free hand inwards to mark 'here' in looking for that edge of the aura. It's somewhat easier, using a pendulum, to learn how to sense that edge directly through your hand, rather than relying on the perhaps over-mechanical nature of the dowsing tool.

Like all our other senses, dowsing is best suited for noticing change rather than continuity. What we understand is this aura or field is something that extends indefinitely, and has many layers and aspects—there's a definite physical layer of trapped heat just above the skin-surface, for example, and another more diffuse layer of body chemicals that we call scent. So we can use the aurameter to show us these layers by giving us slightly different responses for each as we move outward from the body.

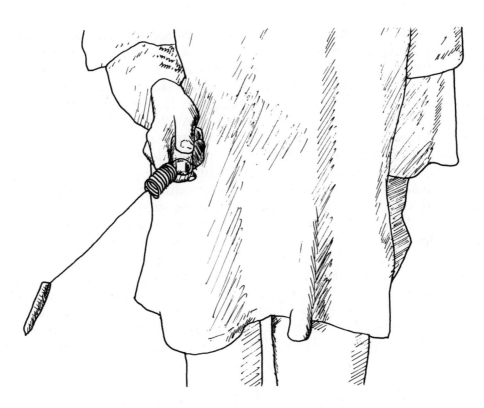

Figure 5.7: Sensing an edge with the Aurameter

Exercise 65: Layers within layers

Imagine that aura around your friend's body: multi-faceted, multi-layered, multi-dimensional. You're using your Aurameter to show the edge at which each layer ends and/or another begins. Move slowly outward from the body, noting the changes and responses of the Aurameter as you move through these interpenetrating fields for a distance of at least 10 to 15 feet. Note carefully where each response occurs; note any differences between them, both in *feel* and in type of response. Do this several times, preferably on different days: see if you can note any correspondences—co-incidences—between the varying shape of those fields within the aura and your friend's general state of health—physical, emotional, mental, and otherwise. Can you see a way to derive meaning from these co-incidences?

Comments:

Watch; observe; think; listen; use all of your senses. When looking at this aura, note any sensory images that stand out—sounds, scents, tastes, tingling feelings in various parts of your body—particularly those that co-incide regularly at the same distance out from your friend's body, or whatever other aura you're looking at. Don't just watch the dowsing rod: watch yourself, how you react.

That's how we build ideas of cause and effect—we watch for co-incidences that occur in some kind of pattern, and interpret meaning accordingly. But because we all see things somewhat differently, we can arrive at the same meaning from quite different co-incidences, so beware of assuming that what makes sense to you will necessarily make sense to anyone else! Make sure that it makes usable sense to *you*: that's what matters.

The best instrument of all

People often ask which dowsing instrument is best. The obvious answer is 'Yes'—all of them or, for that matter, none of them. It all depends on the context. They all have their advantages and disadvantages.

Exercise 66: Which instrument is best?

Of the dowsing instruments we've looked at so far, which one do you prefer? Which one is better for map-dowsing? Which one is best for working outdoors on a windy day? Under what conditions and for what purposes would you choose one instrument rather than another?

_____

Comments:

_____

If you compare your comments on that last exercise with someone else's list, you'll probably find some broad agreement—angle rods are not a good idea in high wind, for example—but no absolute rules about which instrument is best for what. It's a personal choice: there is no best dowsing instrument!

What you'll have seen is that each type of instrument has features which make it useful in specialized areas. There are any number of peculiar dowsing instruments that people have invented to emphasize one function or another: a classic example is the 'radionic box' (see Fig. 5.8), which is, in effect, a specialist dowsing instrument that's designed to work with numbers and patterns. The idea is that different settings of the dials and the general layout of knobs and switches can be used to diagnose and treat illness—the patterns being selected either with a pendulum or, on early versions, a device called a 'stick pad'.

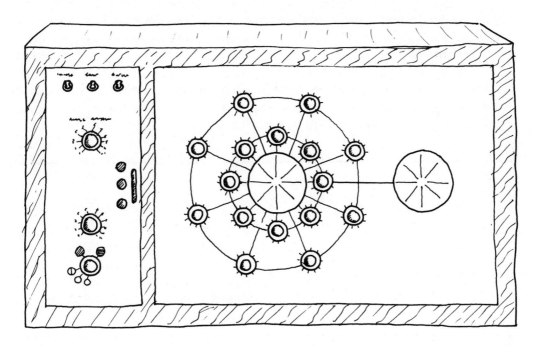

Figure 5.8: The 'radionic box'—one of David Tansley's versions

Some people maintain that the box works—if that's the right word—because the patterns and numbers 'resonate' with the state of the patient, to diagnose illness and restore health. But we can also see that this is much the same idea of resonance that we saw earlier when experimenting with the pendulum. It's a *model*, not a description of cause and effect: we actually don't know how it works. In skilled hands, it does work; in unskilled hands, it doesn't—which is hardly unusual.

The combination of pattern and number is a metaphor or *image* of the state of the patient—in other words we're dealing with something that's image-inary. With the radionic box, as with most other dowsing, we're using images to decide what we're looking for, and then asking the dowsing instrument to help us find it by telling us when where we are co-incides with what we're looking for. It's all co-incidence, mostly image-inary.

We use dowsing instruments to amplify our response to that co-incidence, to make that co-incidence more apparent to our outward senses. And we can amplify that response in any number of ways. So, for the next exercise, try designing your own dowsing tool to resolve a tricky situation.

Exercise 67: The invisible dowsing rod

Dowsing in public can be an embarrassing occupation. Some people stop and stare; others may well think you're some agent of the Devil. So why not invent an invisible dowsing rod? It just has to be something that emphasizes (or at least makes noticeable) some movement of your fingers or hands—but with practice you could probably train any muscle in your body to be 'the dowsing response'. What can you think of to use as a dowsing technique under these circumstances?

Results:

As her solution to this exercise, one of my students came up with a picture postcard, held in a slight curve between her hands. She would wander round a church with the postcard held in prayerful attitude, and would watch the changing reflection from the card's surface as her hands moved relative to each other, changing the curve of the postcard, as her dowsing response.

Another student discovered that he could just rub his finger and thumb together: they would normally pass smoothly over each other, but would stick together when he passed over a water-line or whatever else he was looking for. And another found that her natural response to water, in dowsing mode, was to hiccup. She did look rather strange, though, jerking her neck like an ostrich as she followed a water-line across a field!

What these last 'non-instruments' illustrate is that the dowsing tools don't do the work: *you* do. The spring-rod (or whatever you're using) only *amplifies* the response. Even though it may—and should—feel like it's moving of its own accord, it doesn't respond on its own. The dowsing tools we've looked at do help, but they're only crutches. Ultimately, the best dowsing instrument, the *only* dowsing instrument, is you.

6.

Putting It to Use

We now have our toolkit: so what do we do with it? How do we put that toolkit to use? And, perhaps more to the point, when do we use this dowsers' toolkit rather than any other set of tools?

Quite literally, what's the use? Because dowsing is only useful if we *do* put it to use. In principle we can use dowsing for almost any and every kind of question: but what do *you* actually want to do with it?

So let's apply ourselves to that question.

Apply yourself

Dowsing is always about applying *yourself*, about putting your own inner faculties to better use. Remember, it's not the instrument that does the work, but you. The instrument helps, in marking co-incidences; but you're the one who has to derive some useful meaning from those co-incidences by studying the contexts in which they occur. Without that, it's just coincidence: yet another coincidence.

Coincidences can only be useful if you know how to put them to use. We have to imagine new ways to put them to use; we have to be inventive, to see new ways of finding 'usefulness'. Think of any field of study that interests you, and you'll be able to find some way to use dowsing within it. You can use a pendulum to help select types or quantities of food for a special diet; or use your rod to search for buried artefacts on an archaeological site. It can be useful in searching a library for a specific piece of information, or probing for an awkward intermittent fault in your car. Or, as we've seen, you can plot out weather patterns in advance—you could hardly get it more wrong than the conventional approach, after all . . .

It's all co-incidence: all it takes is a little imagination on your part to work out a way of framing the context, the questions, in such a way that your instrument's rather crude answers can be meaningful. That's what dowsing techniques are all about: ways to describe the context so that you can make sense of those co-incidences at that point at which the instrument responds. It's all co-incidence, it's all image-inary; it's all up to you.

Because it *is* all up to you in the end, I can only give suggestions, some guidelines with which to make a start. The next few chapters give you a variety of examples to play with; once you've put those into practice, you'll have enough understanding of the principles involved to go off on your own, and invent your own ways of dowsing. Apply yourself, in fact.

One gentle warning, though. You could, in principle, apply dowsing techniques to almost every question in life. It's interesting—in fact, good practice—to apply it even to mundane questions: Should I get up now? Do I want this cup of tea? Which movie do I want to watch? And so on. Good practice: but *not* a good way of life, which is what I've seen happen to rather too many would-be dowsers. The pendulum or rod is an extension of your senses, not a replacement for them; and it's certainly *not* a substitute for that rarity called 'common sense'! Once learned, your dowsing is a real skill to be used: but do learn to use it wisely.

Question and Answer

Practical dowsing is all about questions and answers. As we've seen, getting answers from your dowsing instruments is relatively easy: making sense of those answers is not so easy. That's the real skill of dowsing.

Working out what questions to ask, so that you can make sense of the answers your instruments give you, becomes something of a quest. A quest that's made easier, though, because others have been on similar quests in the past, and will often have done much of the hard work for you. Quite a few dowsers have gone to the trouble of building and publishing large sophisticated systems of ready-made questions or sequences of questions, either general-purpose or targeted at a specific field of enquiry such as personal health. (You'll find a few books of this type listed in the Appendix.)

But do always remember that these ready-made systems were devised by someone else for their own specific purposes and, to some extent, biased toward their personal preferences or theories: they may not work in the same way for you or for anyone else, no matter what the author may claim. And each system usually has quirks which make it less than useful on occasion.

Tom Lethbridge, for example, thought that his long-pendulum system, with its regular pattern of 'rates' or pendulum lengths as measured in inches, was universal (and thus, he suggested, proved the primacy of the inch as a unit of measurement). But unfortunately other people, left to their own experiments, come up with different rate values, which means that his system is far from universal: and because of the lengths that Lethbridge used, up to 40 inches, the long-pendulum is not only slow in responding to co-incidences, but has an irritating habit of wrapping itself round your leg as you work.

A nameless Australian author of a book about what he termed 'radial detection' decided that only those people without so-called 'personal disadvantages'—teeth-fillings, scars or eye-glasses—could possibly learn to dowse. Or, more correctly, to learn to use the 'radial detector' (a perfectly ordinary traditional V-rod), since dowsing was, he insisted, strictly the sensation of *physical* radiations, to be interpreted through an immensely complex system of counts of this and movements of that, in a way guaranteed to confuse even those who had no 'personal disadvantages', let alone the rest of us mere mortals. In a later article he announced that he had discovered map-dowsing, but then made a bizarre attempt to explain even *that* in strictly physical terms: something like 'the physical radiations from the place are transmitted to each copy of the map; these copies of the original radiations are thus available to be sensed by the radial detector as it passes over the surface of the map . . . '!

Other people's systems are not always helpful; perhaps especially those you'll find described in books—including this one. There is, however, a useful system that you'll find developed in this book, and that's *your own* system—assuming that you do work through the practical experiments in the exercises, of course. You'll always be developing that system as long as you work with dowsing, adding new ideas here, adapting old techniques to new applications there, or borrowing ideas from someone else's work. Your own system; your own way of working.

You'll have already built up quite a usable system, even at this point in the book. If you look back at what you've done so far, you'll find that you do already know how to go about finding a real hidden object such as a pipe or a cable. All you have to do to find something else is to adapt that experience to the different context. And all that you need for that is a certain amount of 'thinking sideways'—in other words plain ordinary common sense.

Exercise 68: Lost keys

Imagine that you've lost your car keys. How would you go about using your current knowledge of dowsing to help you find them? Which instrument would you prefer to use? Which questions or techniques would you start with? How would you develop your search? What safeguards do you need to use in order not to get sidetracked into searching the wrong place in finer and finer detail?

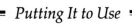

Comments:

If you're in doubt about any part of that exercise, do just look back at what you've done so far. In doing the exercises, you'll have built up enough experience to know how to proceed: you may need to think a little, but you will find that you *do* know what to do.

You know, for example, how to use a 'sample' to represent the bunch of keys: some similar keys, a written note, or just the idea of 'my car keys'. You know how to ask a stream of Yes/No questions: Is it upstairs? Is it in the bedroom? Is it in the closet? And so on. You know how to get your angle rods or a W-rod to point out a direction, if that's an appropriate technique to use. You *know* all this: you've done it already. It may have been in a slightly different context, but you have done it already. All you have to do is adapt existing ideas, existing experience, to a slightly different context, and you'll find that you can invent a usable dowsing technique on the spot.

To illustrate this, let's do something new with our standard example.

Exercise 69: Cracked pipe

You know how to find a pipe by dowsing, using several different instruments and different techniques. Imagine, then, that a leak has developed in that pipe. How would you go about finding that leak? How could you tell how serious it was? How would you make sure that you've found all possible leaks in the pipe? Or, for a trickier exercise, how could you use dowsing techniques to warn for *prospective* leaks— ones that are likely to happen but haven't yet occurred?

Comments:

Once again, you already know how to do all this: if you're in any doubt, go back over the exercises you've already done, and you'll find enough of your own experience to work it out for yourself. The only part that might cause you any difficulty is how to search for a leak: but think of it as a change, a discontinuity in the normal run of the pipe, and use that idea as a sample while you search along the length of the pipe. Remember, it's all image-inary: build an image of what a leak in a pipe would look like, feel like, sound like, smell like, taste like . . . use *that* sense of imagery as your sample.

There's nothing that's actually new in that exercise: it's just a slightly different context, a slightly different sequence of events. Once you understand the *principles* of what you're doing, you can break down almost all new dowsing work that you come across into areas you already know. The only part that would be new, in each case, is a different context and, in some cases, a chance to find a new short-cut that combines several different steps into a single simplified and more elegant technique.

Looking for prospective leaks, for example, is not really any different from looking for prospective weather patterns, which we certainly *have* looked at already: we just combine the time-dowsing techniques of the weather exercise with our experience from the many pipe-search experiments we've done and we have the technique we need. (There's nothing odd or 'paranormal' about using your dowsing to search for likely future leaks, by the way: we do exactly the same if we scan the pipe with, say, ultrasonics or X-rays to show up weak points or corrosion. We don't know *how* our senses merge to give us the equivalent dowsing response, but we do know that, with practice, we can get them to do so: and that's all we need to know at this stage.)

Note that the techniques that you choose to use for those two exercises are likely, even at this stage, to be different from those that other people would select. Check this out, if you can, with someone else who's using this workbook, and you'll see what I mean. It's your choice, your quest: nobody else but you can find what really does work best for you in dowsing. Make a habit of being open, of being willing always to try something new; yet at the same time watch carefully for what *does* work best for you—don't get into changing what works simply for change's sake. Each dowsing answer leads you to a new question: sometimes a new way of phrasing a question, sometimes an old, well-tried way. In learning to dowse better, you learn to know you better, to know your own choices better. And that in itself is a worthwhile exercise!

Meet the Joker . . .

One of the dangers for any newcomer to dowsing (or any other skill, for that matter) is that it works so well at first. For a short while, at least (often only for a *very* short while). In the novelty and excitement of it all, everything seems to go so smoothly, so easily, that it comes as a nasty surprise to find that, quite suddenly, it doesn't work any more. Everything goes wrong. Nothing works. What's happened?

Well, nothing unusual at any rate. This state of 'Why doesn't it work any more?' is just a regular part of the learning process. You've had your share of beginner's luck: now comes the hard work of building the discipline to make it into a real, usable skill that *will* last. So don't give up at this point: but it's time to meet the Joker . . .

LE · MAT

Figure 6.1: Meet the Joker . . .

There's such a regular pattern to the learning process of any skill that it's as if it's being overseen by some strange entity with a very wry sense of humour. A trickster, a Joker, an imaginary deity whose mischievous whims have to be satisfied before we can move on. Not malicious, but certainly idiosyncratic. And capable of pulling some weirdly subtle coincidences on us, to make us see things in a different way. If we don't see things his way . . . well, we hit problems, don't we?

He gives us enough encouragement to get started: then he tests us, all the time. Making things too easy here; making things unnecessarily difficult there. We have to be on our guard throughout a lifetime's practice of a skill: watching, sensing, learning. And ever wary of the Joker!

This Joker is, of course, a personification of some very complex processes within ourselves: but personification, describing those processes as characteristics of some imaginary entity, is a practical way to deal with them. Older cultures used myths of malicious tricksters—the Norse Loki, the Greek Hermes, the native American Coyote, and so on—whilst engineers in even the most advanced technologies of today are painfully aware of the ubiquitousness of what we call Murphy's Law. 'If something can go wrong, it probably will—and usually in the worst possible way': call it God's Own Chaos Department or the workings of some daemon with a strange sense of humour, it all comes out much the same in the end.

The sad part of all this is that it always seems to happen just when we're certain we know how it works. We've just got it *finally* under control when—well, the Joker has different ideas . . .

Exercise 70: Murphy's Law

What's your experience of Murphy's Law? Think of a couple of personal examples, from dowsing or some other skill, especially those where you were quite certain you had things under control. How did you feel when you discovered that things didn't work out as expected?

Comments:

Murphy's Law is best understood as a way of accepting that we can't *ever* have anything truly under control. We can never have complete knowledge; and since we're always learning, we can never have enough skill. We can direct how things happen, but we cannot *control* them, however much we might like to hope or pretend that we can. The difference is subtle but crucial: when the difference does affect your work, it's at best merely embarrassing, at worst disastrous.

Such as drilling a thousand-foot dry well on the basis of unchecked dowsing . . .

One way to cope is to remember that there's a Joker around all the time, watching for you to slip up. If you try to show off, you'll find him right there beside you; if you think you can't do something, he's always willing to prove you right. You learn to be cautious, to expect the unexpected, but with awareness of a wry humour behind it all; you take your work seriously, of course, but never *too* seriously, because the Joker can catch you out that way too. Sometimes he gets really unhelpful, giving you days when *nothing* works: but if you learn to recognize the signs, you can live with that—just accept that that's what's going on, and try again another day. Watch for co-incidences that don't fit the pattern you expect: let your instrument's Idiot response warn you that there's a Joker about!

Another way to deal with the Joker is to catch him in his own trap. Murphy's Law is so much of a law that it also applies to itself most of the time: 'If Murphy's Law can go wrong, it probably will'. So things work not because they're compelled to follow what we think of as rules, but because whatever might encourage them to do otherwise usually goes wrong itself.

Turn Murphy's Law on its head like that, and it suddenly becomes far more useful. A rather backwards way of thinking, perhaps—the twisted logic of the wise fool—but it works. Hence what I call the Fool's Law: 'Things can go right, if you let them go right—especially if you let them go right in unexpected ways'. If we only allow things to go right in expected ways, we're limiting our chances of things going right! We just have to *let* them go right: which isn't as easy as it sounds, because it's all coincidence . . .

Exercise 71: The Fool's Law

Can you think of any personal experiences where things worked out well but in an unexpected way? Did you think at first that things were going wrong? At what point did you recognize that things were actually moving in a more useful direction?

Comments:

Learning to dowse consists of learning to interpret coincidences. Most of the time, it's easiest to follow a system of some kind, giving you a stream of known questions which lead on to new questions depending on what answers you get. But remember that it's *all* coincidence, all co-incidence. Every now and then the Joker will offer you a more useful coincidence: and you'll need the fool's awareness of the Fool's Law to spot it in time.

But there's a very subtle difference between the 'rightness' of the Fool's Law and the more usual blunders when Murphy's Law is at work. These too feel right: but right in a different sense, right because the results would fit our expectations, right because we need them to boost our credibility—in other words a fake 'right' that has a great deal to do with wishful thinking, and little or nothing to do with reality. When we fail to keep in touch with reality, fail to allow for the Joker's games, things can go wrong very quickly.

That's why we need to watch ourselves all the time: it's only by watching ourselves and our results as we work that we can *know* when things are not what they should be. And that's a real part of the skill of dowsing: in some ways *the* skill of dowsing.

Watching yourself

Setting up those questions and interpreting the answers in dowsing is somewhat like programming a computer. Your instruments work in exactly the way you ask them to: no less, no more. And that's why things go wrong.

In a sense, nothing goes wrong: the computer, or dowsing rod, will follow whatever instructions you give it, interpreting them literally, step by step by step. Being machines, they have no idea of whether your instructions make sense or not: they'll just follow them as best they can, to the letter. Hence an often-heard comment from some irate computer programmer: 'Do what I *mean*—not what I say!' Or another common complaint: 'This computer's done exactly what I told it—so what on earth did I tell it to do?'

What's wrong is not the machine, but the instructions. The answers are perfectly correct, in their own way: but if the context of the question is mis-presented, if the question is mis-phrased, it can prevent an answer from making sense—in fact, forces it to be nonsense. If the question's ambiguous, or has internal contradictions of any kind, there's no way you'll get a sensible result. 'Garbage in, garbage out', as the programmers say.

Since dowsing is actually you, *you* are also the context. You're part of the way the question is phrased. Everything you do, everything you think, everything you expect, is part of the context. And that's the hardest part of the context to bring under your direction.

Physical skill, bringing those subtle balances of hand movements into line with your intent, plays an important part, of course. This is true of any other skill: take drawing as an example. When you first start, the hardest part is getting the pencil to do what you want it to do—it jumps around as if it has a mind of its own; it just *will* not go where you want. With time, and with practice—especially practice—the pencil gets the idea, so to speak: it becomes a true extension of you, so anything you want it to do, any texture or line you want it to produce, it will. It's completely under your direction (though never truly under your control: the Joker's always there somewhere . . .). You've mastered the physical skill you need to develop: anything you want to draw, you can. For anything beyond that, you have to develop the artist's eye, selecting what you want to see and show in your drawing: and that isn't a physical skill, but a matter of choice, of awareness, of context, that says more about who you are, your knowledge of yourself, rather than just what you can do with your hands. And, beyond that, the hardest question: *what do you want to do?*

The same is true in dowsing. True, you're unlikely as yet to have full mastery of the physical skills of using the rod or pendulum or whatever, but you're getting there, and getting closer with each bit of practice. It's not that hard. What is hard is watching you: watching your assumptions, your feelings, and, of course, knowing what you want to do.

Exercise 72: Assumptions

(This is a review of an earlier exercise.) Set up to go looking for that pipe again: first, with the assumption that you can't possibly find it; and again, with the assumption that *of course* you can find it, you're perfect, you're the world's best dowser. Note down the difference (if any) between the results. Now do it again, without any specific assumptions: *but see if you can notice what assumptions arise as you search.* Don't worry about them, just notice them: and noticing them, you can allow for their bias in interpreting your results. Watching yourself like this, can you get a sense of being a dispassionate observer, watching you and your assumptions rattling around each other as you work?

Results:

If your dowsing doesn't seem to be working, it isn't because your dowsing isn't working. There's nothing to it: it has no choice but to work, in its limited way. When you get the answers wrong, it's more because you're not watching yourself well enough to see the totality of what's going on, both outside *and* inside you.

And equally, when you get the answers right, it's because you are watching yourself accurately, or perhaps—in the spirit of the Fool's Law—you're at least not getting in the way of letting everything work by itself. Very Zen, that: neither attached to the results, nor detached from them, but *non-attached*. Observing, quietly. In that sense, the accuracy of your dowsing becomes a mirror of how well you're watching your assumptions, the involvement of you in the context of your questing. You watching you watching you, using the totality of your senses as you work.

Bear this in mind as we move on now to some examples of applications of dowsing. Working in dowsing is all about interpretation of co-incidences: not just in what we see in the outer world, but also within ourselves as well, in what we might call image-inary worlds. By watching the *totality* of how these worlds of yours interact, you learn an overall awareness that really does go beyond the simple senses. But remember, behind it all there's a Joker who's always willing to help you make a fool of yourself if you give him half a chance . . . so be wary, and beware!

7.

'Physician, Know Thyself'

By far the most common application of dowsing is not water-divining—which is perhaps what it's best known for—but aspects of personal health and diet: people finding out what works best for their bodies and themselves.

One difficulty arises from this. Dowsing is a good way of learning about yourself, learning how your body reacts to food and environment; but unfortunately, some people seem happiest practising their dowsing on the health of others, which is not such a good idea. Don't. Practice on yourself: then, in time, you just *might* have enough knowledge to work on someone else. Until then, you really can't say that you have the right to do so; and besides, it happens to be illegal in some countries (the United States, for example).

Dowsing techniques, for all their apparent craziness at times, *do* happen to work in this area, so you can do a great deal of damage to someone else if you don't know what you're doing. But you've a perfect right to experiment on yourself: a very worthwhile exercise, as long as you're sensible about it. And since you know your patient (yourself!) intimately, it's by far the easiest way to learn.

'Physician, know thyself.' So let's look at some ways in which dowsing can help in that aim.

Food and drink

You probably have some clear ideas about what food you like, and what kind of foods are good for you—or not so good for you. Some of those ideas are based on practical experience, but some of them may be based on what others have told you, or arise for quite different reasons—the schoolboy aversion to anything green, for example. Your body may have quite different ideas, though: and it's likely to know more about that than you do, at least on a conscious level. So one way to get to know what your body wants, rather than what you *think* it wants, is to ask your dowsing instrument—the pendulum, most often—to help you. To act as an intermediary on your behalf, so to speak.

This is great in theory: but it does depend rather heavily on the accuracy of your dowsing. But looking at it backwards, we can also see this can be a good example of dowsing used to mirror how well you know you. So ask the pendulum to advise you on how to make a cup of tea, and follow its instructions *precisely*. See how well you get on.

Exercise 73: Make a cup of tea

. . . or coffee, if you prefer. Make your basic drink in the usual way, but now use the pendulum to determine how much milk and sugar to add, to your body's preference rather than your usual habits. Hold the milk bottle in one hand, and ask the pendulum to give you a Yes when you've poured enough milk (remember to test before you start pouring—the right answer may be none). Pour until the pendulum tells you to stop (or until the cup's overflowing). Do the same with sugar or sweetener: keep adding it until the pendulum tells you to stop—though once again, remember to check for a possible answer of none. Is the result the same as you would usually make up?

Results:

Whether it's exactly the same as you would normally have, or something that looks utterly revolting, you need to confirm that it's right (in principle!) before you taste it.

Exercise 74: Your body's preference?

Now that you have your cup of tea (or coffee), check it with the pendulum: is this drink going to be good for you? And what question did we *not* ask before making up this drink?

According to the pendulum, this is the drink that your body wants —assuming that it wanted one at all (which is what we didn't check first, of course). So try it: see what it tastes like.

Results:

Don't be dismayed if it's revolting (but then, aren't all medicines supposed to taste that way?). Give yourself some practice: try that exercise again a few more times. It's the perfect direct feedback on the quality of your dowsing . . .

Once you're a little happier about this—or at least fairly certain that you're not going to poison yourself—move on to a something a little larger.

Exercise 75: The dowser's school of cookery

Make a pie or an omelette. Leave your common sense and previous experience at the kitchen door, and instead rely entirely upon your dowsing to tell you what to put into it, and how much of each item to put into it, as with your tea or coffee in the last exercise. Do keep in mind that you want this to be enjoyable to eat! After you've added an item to the mix, ask your rod or pendulum whether something else should be added and, if so, to point to it. Keep adding more ingredients until your dowsing tells you to stop. And cook the dish at the temperature your dowsing suggests, for the length of time that your dowsing suggests. Anything interesting happen? What's the result like?

Results:

Having practised in the home, now try the same out in the big wide world, outside of your control. Before you do, it's a good idea to practise the use of one of the 'invisible' instruments and techniques we saw in Chapter 5, so that you can dowse in public places such as restaurants without feeling embarrassed.

Exercise 76: What's on the menu?

Go out for a meal, preferably in a foreign restaurant where they don't translate the names and contents of the dishes. Use whatever dowsing technique you like to select your meal, with the idea in mind of 'find me something that I'll like'. Point to each entry on the menu, asking your pendulum for a Yes response to a dish that you'd like: remember to check the whole menu, don't just stop at the first Yes. Note the variations in response: a half-hearted Yes to one item, a vague non-committal No for another, perhaps even an Idiot response. Interpret these responses as best you can, and place your order. What did you end up with? Was it a surprise? Did you enjoy it?

_____

Results:

_____

For a variant on the same theme, use your dowsing to help you select something from the menu which is not only tasty but also low in calories. What we're doing here is dowsing using a two- part 'sample'—'both tasty *and* low in calories'—and asking the pendulum to come up with what it (in other words your own unconscious) considers the best compromise. The sample here would either be an idea in your mind, or, perhaps easier, a note written on paper. Remember that you're using it to remind you that you want a Yes response to coincide with your pointing at the item on the menu that's the best *compromise* to your request, as given in the sample.

Exercise 77: Weight-watchers

Go to a restaurant, or perhaps the supermarket ready-meals section, and use your dowsing to pick out something that's both tasty *and* low in calories. What did you get? Or did you only get an Idiot response?

Results:

You can, of course, add more parts to the sample—such as 'and please, not *another* salad!'—but it does restrict your options. If you only get an Idiot response from your dowsing, you'll have to be less choosy—drop a part from that compound sample, and try again.

Exercise 78: Yellow Pages

If you're fortunate enough to have a range of restaurants in your area, use your dowsing to select one from the list in the telephone book. Watch your thinking, to make sure that your usual preconceptions— 'but I don't *like* Indian food . . . '—don't get in the way: if necessary, cover up the restaurant names and just use your dowsing to pick one by telephone number alone. Go there; pick the dishes by dowsing too. What was this all-done-by-dowsing meal like?

Comments:

If nothing else, it's one way to become a little more adventurous in your eating habits!

Personal health

One of the drawbacks of eating out in strange restaurants is the uncertainty about whether you're likely to ruin an enjoyable evening out by following it with a distinctly unenjoyable bout of food poisoning. The doubt is always there: even if the cooking's excellent, your body may just decide to complain, in no uncertain terms, about the unfamiliarity of it all.

Exercise 79: 'I like it, but will it like me?'

Use your dowsing to check foods in restaurants and shops, to see whether they would disagree with you or, for that matter, to see whether they're the best available. Use a variety of ideas as samples, such as 'Is there anything in this that would upset my body?', 'Is this the freshest/best' or 'Will these be ripe at the time I plan to use them?', and the like. Do the results differ from your usual judgements of the quality of foods available?

Comments:

Note too the inevitable trade-offs: the best is rarely the cheapest, and so on. But this is where watching the detail of your instrument's responses, from the barely-more-than-Neutral to the unquestionably emphatic Yes or No, can really help, showing you the best compromises for the *total* set of limits that you give it to work with. The total list for that compound sample that you're using to control the dowsing with can end up surprisingly long: 'the freshest *but* the ones that will still be fresh when I want them *and* the most nutritious for me *and* the best price *and* in one of the shops where I like spending my money because the others are a bunch of greedy thieves . . . '—notice how preconceptions can creep in too!

A lot of food, whether from a restaurant or a supermarket, will have a variety of additives in it. These are all there for perfectly good reasons, as far as the suppliers are concerned: some are essential to keep the food fresh, some are required mainly because the food has to have a long shelf-life, and others are needed to make the food marketable—sulphur dioxide to prevent dried fruits going brown, for example.

In theory, none of these additives are harmful: but in practice, most could well be so for a very small minority, and a few could be politely described as 'dubious' for most of us—some are known to be linked to hyperactivity in children, for example. Even if it does only affect a tiny minority, you never know if you're going to be one of that 'tiny minority': statistics will tell you the probability, perhaps, but can't tell you if it will affect *you*. But your body knows—and can tell you if you know how to ask it. So, this is another application for your dowsing.

Exercise 80: E is for Additive

All legally-permitted food additives are either named on the packet or coded by an 'E' number, such as E201 or E103. Find a copy of *E For Additives*, or some other book that gives an ordered list of additives. Using a pendulum or some other dowsing technique that allows you to point, work your way down the list with a question such as 'Is this good for me when used in the usual way in food?' (Note: don't ask 'Is this bad for me?'. That's a classic example of a double-negative, in which No can mean either 'it's not bad' or 'it is negative for me'—in other words bad for you. Take care!). For most, expect a Neutral or a non-committal response either way. Note down those for which you get a clear Yes, No, or Idiot. Check the results against the book. Anything interesting?

Results:

We've looked at additives only in a general way here: as usual, it's the *context* in which they're used that matters. Sulphur dioxide isn't exactly good for you on its own—it's poisonous, in fact—but has been used for centuries as a very necessary and effective preservative. If you're interested in avoiding certain additives, check not just the product label, but check again with your dowsing: the context in which one of your 'bad' additives is used, mixed up with everything else in the jar, may actually be good medicine for you at times!

Much the same applies to allergies. It is, however, another area that's been blown up way out of proportion. Most of us have minor allergies to something or other: certain milk products, to give one example. And it usually doesn't much matter. We mostly learn the hard way that some things are best avoided, however much we might like them. But it's often hard to work out just what it is that's affecting us adversely: so, once again, we can use our dowsing to help:

Exercise 81: . . . and A is for Allergies

A very common type of allergic reaction is that 'bloated' feeling after even a light meal with the wrong kind of food in it. Next time you feel heavy or lethargic like that after a meal, write down as complete a list as you can remember of everything you've just eaten. Now use your dowsing to go through the list, using a question such as 'Is this responsible for my current discomfort?' Note that it may be the *combination* of two or more items (strawberries and mustard?) or the *quantity* (an entire jar of pickled onions?) that's the key issue—again, watch for Idiot responses and other tell-tale clues. Over a period of time, compare your notes from several occurrences: does a regular pattern begin to emerge?

Comments:

Here you're using your dowsing in a truly scientific manner: recording, comparing, assessing in an objective way—or at least as objective as you can be when you're also the subject of your experiments. Note, though, that the results will probably apply only to *you*, and even then perhaps only for a limited period of time. You change; your body changes with you; and its ability to tolerate doubtful substances will vary with circumstances anyway. So don't expect any hard and fast rules to come out of these experiments: just use them as a way to learn more about yourself.

The same could be said for another kind of additives that are often over-used, namely vitamins and dietary supplements. I'm not keen on them—apart from anything else, they're fiendishly expensive—but many of my friends swear by their breakfast-time session with those pills and potions. You may have bottles and jars by the dozen, but your

Figure 7.1: '. . . that breakfast-time session with pills and potions . . .'

needs will vary every day: so which ones do you choose from? Once more, your dowsing skills can come to the rescue.

Exercise 82: Vitamins

Assuming you have a set of vitamins or dietary supplements, lay the bottles out in a line. Point to each in turn with your dowsing instrument, asking 'Do I need some of the contents of this jar today?' or some such question. Note again the varying responses: for many you'll get a non-committal answer, for some you'll get a definite Yes, for others an equally definite No. (Or Idiot, of course—in which case it's time to re-think somewhat). For each bottle for which you have a definite Yes, use your dowsing to select the quantity ('Do I need another?' and so on). Record the results over a period of time. Do you notice any difference in general health? Have you saved money by using only the vitamins your dowsing has suggested you need?

Comments:

It's probably well worth doing the same with that bewildering array on display in the pharmacy or health-food store.

Exercise 83: Pick your own

Use your dowsing to help you choose vitamins and dietary supplements from the store. (It's probably best to use an 'invisible' dowsing technique for this.) Go down the rows, asking 'Do I need what's in this jar (or whatever)?' If you're certain that you want Vitamin C, for example, use your dowsing to select which one of the many on the shelves to buy, or for that matter which one is the best value as far as your body's concerned—but watch for an Idiot response, which would suggest that you don't *need* Vitamin C. How do you get on?

Results:

By keeping in mind the idea of 'best *value*', and including it in the compound 'sample' that you use with your dowsing, you should actually save money, too. Well worth a try, anyway.

To go much beyond this with dowsing we start to move into the more fraught realms of diagnosis and prescription, which it is not appropriate to discuss in a book of this type. There are legal problems, as I mentioned earlier; and there's also the real risk of doing yourself some damage if your dowsing's not as good as you might hope it is. Preconceptions can get in the way far too easily . . .

But we can at least play with some ideas. And one group of 'non-medicines' that immediately come to mind for this are the Bach Remedies—essences of 38 different flowers, so much diluted that they're themselves best described as ideas rather than medicines. Like dowsing, there's nothing to them: it's all co-incidence—whatever that may mean. And, like dowsing, we can put co-incidence to practical use.

In Edward Bach's original concept, these flower essences could be used to relieve a wide variety of forms of mental or emotional stress. Bach maintained that physical illness was the outward result of inner stress: so by helping the inner states to stabilize themselves, with the aid of the Remedies, outer illness is freed to sort itself out on its own. It's an interesting idea, and one that has many protagonists.

The Remedies themselves are made by steeping the respective flowers in water, and then diluting the result many times, in a manner similar to homoeopathic remedies. To use a Remedy, you'd select one (or more) by identifying the symptoms from the chart below, and placing a single drop of the respective Remedy either under the tongue, or onto a small sugar tablet to be swallowed in the usual way.

Table 7.1: The Bach Remedies: a summary

Rock Rose	*Fear:* terror, panic, fear in extreme
Mimulus	*Fear:* shyness, timidity, fears with known origin
Cherry Plum	*Fear:* collapse of mental control, vicious temper, fear of doing harm to others
Aspen	*Fear:* apprehension, foreboding, vague fears with unknown origin
Red Chestnut	*Fear:* over-caring and exaggerated fears for others (especially loved ones), anticipates 'the worst'
Cerato	*Uncertainty:* doubts own judgement, often misguided, seeks guidance from authority-figures
Scleranthus	*Uncertainty:* indecision, vacillation, fluctuating moods
Gentian	*Uncertainty:* despondent, easily discouraged, dejected from known cause
Gorse	*Uncertainty:* extreme hopelessness, despair, pessimism, negativity, fatalism
Hornbeam	*Uncertainty:* procrastination, (but once started task is usually finished)
Wild Oat	*Uncertainty:* unfulfilled, ambitious but aimless
Clematis	*Avoiding here and now:* day dreaming, indifference, inattention, escapism
Honeysuckle	*Avoiding here and now:* nostalgia, reflecting on past pleasures and glories, homesickness
Wild Rose	*Avoiding here and now:* resignation, apathy, drifting, no ambition
Olive	*Avoiding here and now:* complete exhaustion, drained of energy, everything is a chore
White Chestnut	*Avoiding here and now:* preoccupied with persistent unwarranted worries, mental arguments

Mustard	*Avoiding here and now:* deep gloom, melancholia, recurrent depression for no known reason
Chestnut Bud	*Avoiding here and now:* unobservant of life's lessons, repeats same mistakes
Water Violet	*Loneliness:* clean living, proud, reserved, sedate, sometimes 'superior aloof', capable, independent, reliable
Impatiens	*Loneliness:* impatient (especially with others), hasty, independent, 'can't wait' quickness
Heather	*Loneliness:* over-concerned with self, talkative bores, poor listeners, hates to be alone
Agrimony	*Oversensitivity:* facade of cheerfulness hides inner torture, hides worries from others
Centaury	*Oversensitivity:* weak-willed, subservient, over anxious to please, 'doormat' tendency, easily exploited
Walnut	*Oversensitivity:* overwhelmed by powerful influences at present time—normally capable
Holly	*Oversensitivity:* misanthropy, envy, jealousy, hatred, suspicion
Larch	*Despondency and despair:* no confidence, expects and fears failure, does not try, unwarranted sense of inferiority
Pine	*Despondency and despair:* guilt, self reproach, over conscientiousness, feels unworthy, takes blame for others' mistakes
Elm	*Despondency and despair:* temporarily overwhelmed by responsibility, normally very capable
Sweet Chestnut	*Despondency and despair:* extreme anguish, desolation, at limit of emotional endurance (non-suicidal)
Star of Bethlehem	*Despondency and despair:* effect of fright, serious news, great sorrow, trauma etc
Willow	*Despondency and despair:* resentment, bitterness, self pity
Oak	*Despondency and despair:* at limit of endurance against illness and/or physical adversity
Crab Apple	*Despondency and despair:* feels unclean (in mind or body), self-dislike/disgust
Chicory	*Overcare:* selfishness, possessiveness, demands respect and obedience
Vervain	*Overcare:* over enthusiastic, fanatical, highly strung, incensed by injustices
Vine	*Overcare:* domineering, inflexible, ambitious, tyrannical/autocratic
Beech	*Overcare:* intolerant, critical, arrogant, judgemental

| **Rock Water** | *Overcare:* self-denial, rigid, tight, self-righteous, aims to set an example |

Avoiding here and now: Bach's original term was 'Lack of interest in present circumstances'.

Oversensitivity: Bach's original term was 'Oversensitivity to influences and ideas'.

Overcare: Bach's original term was 'Overcare for others' welfare'.

The *Rescue Remedy*—for emergencies and accidents—is a combination of Cherry Plum, Clematis, Impatiens, Rock Rose and Star of Bethlehem.

According to Bach, if a remedy is not needed, it is simply ignored by the body: so in principle you can't do any harm to yourself by mis-selecting one. It's a good thing: many people consume vast amounts of the 'Rescue Remedy'—supposedly reserved for emergencies only—on an everyday basis . . . Life may be hard, but we do need to be more sensible than that about our use of medicines!

The Bach Remedies chart is useful here, though, because it gives us another list on which to practise our dowsing.

Exercise 84: Bach remedies

This is another longer-term exercise. Cover the 'symptoms' part of the Bach Remedies chart with a flap of paper, leaving only the flower names visible. Over a period of at least 10 days, note down each day, at a regular time, a summary of what you think of as your current mental or emotional state. Then use your preferred list dowsing technique to select any (or none) of the remedies with which to 'treat' yourself for that day. Assume that a Yes would mean that you would in principle be appropriate to give yourself a dose of that remedy (doing so is not a requirement for the exercise!); a definite No indicates the 'positive' aspect of that mental state—a No for Larch would suggest a high degree of confidence, for example. At the end of the test period, compare your notes. How well do they match up?

Results:

Because it's hard being objective about your own feelings and emotional states, you may find it easier to do this with a friend: but *don't* do it without their agreement. (That would be an invasion of privacy: definitely *not* something I'd want to encourage.) Record your own state as best you can, while going through the list working out choices of remedies for your friend. At the end of the period, compare notes; see what you get.

You could, if you like, try actually using the Bach remedies for yourself: that's up to you. If you do, once again be scientific about it: record your choices, and any co-incidental changes in your emotional state that you notice. That way you'll have a precise record of the accuracy—and usefulness—of your dowsing.

But in another experiment you could try, we go all the way with assuming that the Bach remedies are indeed 'only' ideas, and imagine that it's the *idea* of the remedy, rather than the (barely?) physical remedy itself, that does the work. Since it's all co-incidence and mostly image-inary, we move straight into a magical realm, of ideas and images being put to practical use.

Exercise 85: Magician, heal thyself

Go through the list of remedies each day as before, dowsing for those that would help your current emotional state. But rather than taking a dose of the remedy, just write out its name on a piece of paper. If appropriate, write a list of several flower names on that piece of paper. If you have a definite No for a given flower name, write down that it's not needed: 'No Holly needed', for example. Fold up the piece of paper, put it in your wallet or purse, carry it round with you as a kind of talisman. Do this, again, for at least 10 consecutive days: note down your changes in emotional states. What results do you notice?

_____

Results:

_____

However it works, it's certainly co-incidence, and it's entirely image-inary. Magic! The Fool's Law again: if you *let* it work, it works—a magical approach to the technology of health.

But a little knowledge of magic can be a dangerous thing. There's a tortuous paradox which says "Things have not only to be seen to be believed, but often have to be believed to be seen'. You can use magical tricks to create real positive change in your health; but you can also imagine yourself ill until you really *are* ill, if that's what you really want . . . the hypochondriac's delight! In that sense you are, quite literally, responsible for your own health: so do be sensible when experimenting in this strange and often confusing area.

Trust your senses

One way things can go wrong with these games is if you let your mind wander off on its own, following some idea or theory, without remaining in full contact with the rest of the body. Dowsing is about linking all our senses *together* and making use of that overall awareness: not about drifting off into pointless—and perhaps potentially danger-ous—mind-games, lost in each and every fashionable fad or fantasy. This is particularly true of the whole arena of diet and personal health.

So at this point it's worth while returning to a theme we looked at in Chapter 5, about learning to watch your overall sensing rather than relying solely upon the mechanical nature of the dowsing tools. The dowsing provides the focus, somewhere precise and narrow to place your attention: but much of the actual work is done by observing, by being aware, being wide open to other possibilities, other useful co-incidences. It's what I call 'thinking narrow, *being* wide'.

Exercise 86: A wider awareness

Go back to the two 'aura' exercises in Chapter 5 (Exercise 64 'First find your aura' and Exercise 65, 'Layers within layers'). Do them again, but this time pay particular attention to what you *feel* about the source of those auras, whatever it is. Use your dowsing as a focus for your attention, but keep your awareness wide. Try finding these image-inary auras around your jars of vitamins and dietary supplements: what do you find? What do you sense?

Comments:

Most of our attention, most of the time, is focused on vision: interpreting what we *see*. Sometimes it's easier to observe with a wider awareness if we move the focus of attention to some other sense. Most of our dowsing depends on touch—feeling those subtle movements of rod or pendulum—so, for a change, focus attention instead on your sense of smell.

Exercise 87: Follow your nose

Go back to the vitamins exercise earlier in this chapter (Exercise 82) and set up as before: but this time use your nose, your sense of smell, as your dowsing instrument. Focus your attention on your sense of smell. Allow it to register more than just the basic smell of each substance: go deeper, sense wider. Sniff gently over each jar; see which ones smell the most interesting. Compare the results with your previous dowsing experiments; note how the jars you pick out as the most 'interesting' will vary from day to day. Can you see any regular pattern developing—matching your changing moods, for example?

Comments:

It's not easy at first: all our training, at school and beyond, is about *thinking*, not about sensing—and particularly not about *trusting* those senses of our own. We're not supposed to judge for ourselves: the authorities, whoever they were, always knew better.

That may be valid in the outer world: there are always specialists who perhaps do know more than the rest of us (though sometimes it's doubtful . . .). But when it comes to knowing *you*, the only possible 'true authority' must be you. Especially if you've learned how to observe you, how to know you. So watch how the totality of you responds to something:

Exercise 88: Keep in touch

Set up to do the vitamins exercise again. This time use neither your dowsing as such, nor your nose, but your *overall* awareness. Reach out, touch each of the jars in turn. What do you sense? What do they say to you (metaphorically speaking)? Don't try, just let your senses reach out: remember that Zen idea of 'doing no-thing'. Pass your hands over the jars: do you feel anything, is there any particular 'pull' to one or another? Look at them, casually: do any of them stand out in any way, or seem more noticeable? Is there any sense of a sound coming from any of the jars? Just let an overall awareness build up; learn to trust your senses. What can you learn from this depth of observation?

Comments:

You may well feel a little childish doing this. That's fine: just go along with it. The 'childish and silly' feeling comes because this goes counter to almost everything we're taught in school and beyond, but that's fine too. You're learning a *skill* here, not someone else's ideas about how things are supposed to work. Since it's all co-incidence and mostly image-inary, it doesn't really matter *what* we choose to believe, as long as it does the job well: and you're the best one to find out how things really *do* work best for you.

In fact, once we can accept that it really *is* all co-incidence and mostly image-inary, we can go all the way back, full circle, and just play magical games with co-incidence instead.

Exercise 89: It was a good idea at the time . . .

Stop thinking, and just pick up one of the vitamin jars. At random. Now—without thinking—do you want one of the pills from this jar today? Yes or No (or Idiot)—quick! Don't give yourself time to think! Restrict your thinking to a single idea: 'Today's vitamins . . . ' and let your body-knowledge do the rest. Or go back to an earlier exercise and make your omelette the same way: Quick! Without thinking! Do I want this cheese in my omelette? Yes or No (or Idiot)—quick! Do it *fast*: can you go beyond panic, into a state where you simply *know*?

Results:

This takes us back to a very old concept, now all but forgotten: something that used to be called 'providence', or, quite literally, 'provide-ence'. That's just co-incidence too: in this case, letting your inner knowledge guide you to the right coincidences to match your needs in the moment. It works. When you *let* it work—which isn't easy.

One of the best ways to use dowsing is as a gateway into learning this kind of inner knowledge. A way to become aware of your own choices: not other people's choices, or other people's assumptions, but *your own* choices, your own body's awareness of itself and its interaction with its environment.

So: Physician, *know* thyself!

8.

Finding Out

After our foray into the inner worlds of health and diet, it's time to return to the outer world and the more traditional application of dowsing, namely *finding* things.

The outside world

In principle you could use dowsing to help you find anything, as long as you can describe it. There are many historical references to dowsing, but it's interesting to note that the first instruction book on practical dowsing—part of Agricola's *De Re Metallica* in the sixteenth century—was about its use in mining, searching for coal and tin and other minerals: water divining, in the modern sense, came somewhat later. And dowsing for mines worked well, too: the deep Cornish tin-mines were opened up in the late sixteenth century by dowser-engineers brought over from Belgium.

The dowsers of that time used simple but effective techniques, holding a sample of tin (or whatever they were looking for) in one hand while holding a wooden V-rod. It was strictly field-dowsing, walking backwards and forwards, plotting out seams of ore with markers on the ground. This can be laborious, so we can now do some of the preliminary searches on a map instead:

Exercise 90: Minerals on the map

We want to plot out the shape and position relative to the surface of a mineral seam, so choose a mineral that's known to be present under-ground in your area: copper, coal, iron ore or whatever. (An alternative in some areas, such as California, would be underground faults). First choose some way of describing what you're looking for: either a sample, or a written reference, or whatever works best for you (for a fault, use the idea of *discontinuity* in the underlying rock-structure). Do make sure that you're looking for something significant in size: you do want to ignore the little discontinuities and tiny pieces of mineral (especially as trash, such as beer cans) that you can find almost everywhere. Then, using your sample as your reference point ('I'm looking for *this*'), move over the map with an instrument such as a pendulum or miniature angle rods: start from one edge of the map, asking for the instrument to show you a *change* which corresponds to where the seam or fault starts or ends. (Note that dowsing, for well-understood perceptual reasons, is good at noticing change, but is *not* good at picking up continuity: if the seam is horizontal and runs under the entire area of the map, you may not recognize that it's there at all. If you have no luck, try an alternative mineral, or look for fault-lines, which *do* occur as lines at the surface.) Using either a directional technique or a series of passes over the map, plot out an edge that marks the course of the seam or fault. Repeat this in various places across the map.

Comments:

If you're looking for minerals—or, as we'll see later, water—it's obviously going to be important to find out, before you'd do any digging, how far down you'd have to go to get to it, and whether what you'd find is going to be worth finding anyway.

Exercise 91: Minerals—how deep, how much

Use a variety of techniques to assess the depth and quality of a mineral seam that you've found on the map. The scale is likely to be too small to make the Bishop's Rule usable: try a series of number questions such as 'Is it more than 100/200/500 feet down?', 'Is the mineral yield likely to be less than 10%/1%/0.1% of the total rock?' and so on. How detailed a picture of the underground structure can you build up?

Results:

Remember that since we're using the map only as a diagram or *representation* of the landscape, we can also use alternative ways to represent 'here', the place where we're looking with our dowsing.

Figure 8.1: Building a cross-section from the map

One example of an alternate view is a cross-section, looking at the land vertically rather than horizontally:

Exercise 92: Minerals—looking sideways

Draw a line on the map to mark the line of the cross-section that you're about to construct. Draw a single straight line at the top of a piece of blank paper—for simplicity, make it the same length as your map line. Mark off a series of divisions along this top line—at ¼" intervals, perhaps. State that you're going to use a specific vertical scale, such as one inch per hundred feet down. Place a ruler on the paper, marking a vertical line downward from the first of the horizontal division marks. Using a pencil as both pointer and marker, ask your pendulum to indicate each discontinuity or change of geological layer as you run your pencil downward past the scale representation of that point. Remember to make it clear to yourself that this is a cross-section at the surface position *represented* by the respective point on the line that you've marked on the map. Repeat this for each of your horizontal division marks, to build up a plot of the layers of discontinuity beneath the surface along the map line. Do your plot-points seem to join up into definite layers (remember that the layers may well *not* be horizontal)? Can you determine what rock-type each layer is composed of? What other information can you derive from your cross-section?

Results:

Once you're comfortable with your results (look to that inner knowing, that inner overall sensing, as a check), go out to the actual site and try to confirm it on the ground.

Exercise 93: Minerals on the ground

Go to an area that you've picked out as interesting on your map, and, without comparing with your map dowsing, do a similar survey on the ground for the same type of mineral or discontinuity. Use the same sample as in the previous exercise, with the usual range of field techniques to do your search: direction, shape, 'X marks the spot', and so on. Keep in touch with the ground, with the physical sense of here and now, as much as possible: use 'non-contact' techniques such as 'let your eyes do the walking' only where you have to. How closely do your two surveys match? How much does the fact of being *in* the landscape, rather than working only on an image of it, make a difference to your sense of certainty about your results, and to the results themselves?

Comments:

So far in this set of exercises, it's all been dowsing—which, as we know, is entirely coincidence and mostly imaginary. We now have to make sure that our results from those image-inary senses actually have coincided with what we were looking for in the physical world. In other words, now you think you've found something, prove it.

Exercise 94: Minerals—check your results

Take your two sets of survey data to your local library, and check them against published reference works such as the Geological Survey maps of the area, which should show all significant known mineral deposits and faults, with both surface and (usually) some cross-section representations. How well do your results match up? If your surveys gave different results, was your dowsing more accurate on the map or in the field? Can you recall any images or senses that came up while dowsing which make more sense now that you have someone else's results to compare with? Or did you find any direct confirmation—such as actual mines or mining debris—during your field survey?

Comments:

In the end, dowsing is only useful if you can use it. These exercises we've just done are a very practical example of how you can put your dowsing to use—and there are indeed a number of professional dowsers who make their living from that kind of work. With enough practice, you could join them too . . .

Water divining

This leads us on to the search for another substance, the one we most often associate with dowsing: water.

Everyone's heard of water divining. The classic stereotype of the dowser is an old man looking for water with a forked stick in the backwoods somewhere, calling on strange and magical forces to help him in his search. Those times may have passed, but the need for water most certainly hasn't: there's probably a greater need for good water-finders now than at any time in history.

Despite what geologists' organizations would have us believe, 'scientific' geology isn't anything like the only technique used to find water these days. There are plenty of professional dowsers around, even (or especially) in so-called 'advanced' countries. And unlike geologists, many of them work on the basis of 'no water, no pay'—including the horrendous cost of drilling a well—which means they have to be *very* certain about what they know and what they don't. Which is more than can be said for some geological reports . . .

I've often heard geologists argue that dowsing is simply *wrong*: water just doesn't flow in pretty little underground streams, which is what they hear dowsers talking about. As usual, the problem arises from the point of view. Geologists, on the one hand, see things in terms of structure, in terms of continuity, of a 'water table' trapped between layers of permeable and impermeable rock. But the dowsers—as you'll have found from your own experiments—see things in terms of *dis*continuity, of edges and points and lines. And that means that we see water in terms of *edges* of flow, for which the idea of a 'water line' or 'underground stream' is a convenient—and even, in some fractured rocks, accurate—shorthand notation. Both models are tools in a conceptual toolkit: so it doesn't matter which approach is true, because in a sense both and neither of them are true. What matters is which one is useful.

The short answer, of course, is that both are 'true', *depending on the circumstances*: which is why good professional water-dowsers do know a great deal about geology, and why it's a pity that so few geologists take dowsing seriously. If you're looking for water, the geologists' kind of model is useful where you *do* have water held in a reservoir between simple layered rock structures—the London basin is one example. But it's not much use if the local geology is a mess, as it is in the eastern part of Somerset or the earthquake zones of California, for example, because the water's always moving, flowing from place to place. In those areas we need a perceptual model to pick out points and lines of flow, and preferably to find just *one* place on the surface corresponding with a concentration of water-flows below—what dowsers would call a 'knot' of water-lines. That's the sort of water-finding work for which dowsing is best suited. And it's not easy, even then.

To start with, we have to look for a water line.

Exercise 95: Water—first find your line

Set yourself up to look for underground water. You know how to find a water pipe: it's exactly the same, except that you're looking for a *natural* flow beneath your feet. There are little trickles of water everywhere underground, of course, but we want more than that: you're looking for a concentration of underground water, which we can think of as a flow or line of water—a 'water line'. Hold an actual sample of local spring water, perhaps; image what you're looking for as 'like a pipe, but not a pipe'. Start off by looking around your house—you should know where the pipes are by now!—or, if necessary, cast your net a little wider. Working either on a map or in the field, or both, what kind of results do you get? How do you distinguish between water in a pipe, and a water-flow that's *not* in a pipe?

Results:

There really *is* a difference in feel, in the overall sense, of pipe water and free-flowing water. It may take you a little while to be certain of the difference: but then it probably took you (may still be taking you!) a little time to get the knack of using the dowsing instruments themselves. If it isn't clear at the moment, just be patient, and keep practising: it will come in time.

One cross-check is to compare the depth of this water line with that of a pipe.

Exercise 96: Water—now find the depth

You have a variety of depthing techniques at your disposal: Bishop's Rule, walking 'downwards' on the spot, asking a sequence of Yes/No questions, or anything else you've invented. Go back to your usual water pipe, and check the depth there, to calibrate your dowsing; now go to one point on your new water line, and use the same technique to find the depth. Ask for the depth of the water line, not that of the pipe! If it's a water-flow in rock, it may spread over a considerable range in depth, giving you several effective depths—the start, the end, the centre of the flow. Which depth is the best? And best in what sense?

Comments:

Another cross-check is to compare the amount of water in the two flows: pipe and water line. This is a little tricky with the pipe, since the water-flow depends on whether or not the tap has been turned on; but the flow in an underground seam is fairly constant from moment to moment, changing with the weather and the seasons. So, how much water is available?

Exercise 97: Water—how much is there?

As with the last exercise, choose from your toolkit a technique to count quantities: Yes/No questions again, or counting turns of a pendulum, or some such. With some regular unit such as gallons per hour in mind, use your dowsing to check the water-flow in the pipe when the tap is open, and when it's closed (you should get a result of zero for that, of course). Now try measuring the flow—not the amount of water, but the *flow*, the amount of water available over time. What result do you get? What difference in results do you get if you use time dowsing—image-ining yourself doing the same test at a different time from 'now'—in other seasons: summer, winter, last year, next year?

Results:

Water isn't just water: it comes in many variations of quality as well as quantity. What you have below you could be the purest spring water, or unusable surface water contaminated with industrial or farm waste, sewage, or worse. It could be either beneficial or harmful to health in a quite different, more image-inary sense—something dowsers call 'white' or 'black' water. So: what have you found?

Exercise 98: Water—is it any good?

Again, you have a range of techniques that you know how to use: assess the quality of what you've found, standing at that point above your water line. Or try another technique: assess its potability in terms of shades of grey, with white as the purest and black as unusable. Or invent other techniques: see what you can do. Keep in mind an image of this water moving below you: feel it, sense it. What's it like? What are its qualities?

Comments:

In practice, we don't want just any place above the water line: we need to find the *best* place to drill a well. An ideal place would be one where many lines come together or cross over each other: there we can tap the water from several flows rather than just one. See what you can find.

Exercise 99: Water—follow the lines

Angle rods are probably best for this exercise. Go to your point above the water line, and ask the rods to follow the direction of flow. Follow it as best you can. Take note of junctions (where one rod points to one side, while the other points ahead) or crossings (rods point either side for a moment, and then return to the main track). Watch out particularly for a 'knot', where several lines meet or cross (you may find your rods leading you in circles there—hence the alternate term 'blind spring'). Having found this knot-point, do all your previous tests: depth(s), quantity, quality. Would this be a good place to drill a well? How reliable would the supply be?

Comments:

The key to water divining is to be able to put all these parts together in one operation, and *know* when you have a worthwhile supply of water below you.

But in a way, that's only the start. You then have to prove it the hard way, by getting someone else to drill down at the exact spot you've selected, at the exact depth you specify. Even that's not easy: the drill will wander off line all too often in many types of strata—so you not only have to know that it's happened, but to know what to tell the operating crew to do about it. And so on: that's why professional water-finding has always been so much of a skill, and why it's *not* a sensible part of dowsing for beginners to experiment with much more than we've done so far. To go further, you'll really need the old-fashioned master-apprentice system, rather than a simple Workbook like this one. If you want to learn more, your best bet would be to contact the national dowsing societies, whose addresses are in the Appendix.

Hide and seek

One application of dowsing that's not so fraught with risks as water divining is the old game of hide-and-seek: finding some*one* rather than some*thing*. It's also a good example of how we can put map- and time-dowsing to practical use.

It also gives us a chance to introduce another way of working with a map, namely using a kind of coordinate technique.

You'll need a friend to help you with the exercises in this section. The idea is that you should be able to find their position, as represented by the map, at a particular point in time—and space, of course—by finding a pair of coordinates that would mark that point on the map. As your friend moves around, you should be able to plot their changing position on the map. The pendulum is by far the best tool for this type of work.

Exercise 100: Where are they now?

Set a map of your local area out on the table, as in Figure 8.2. Build in

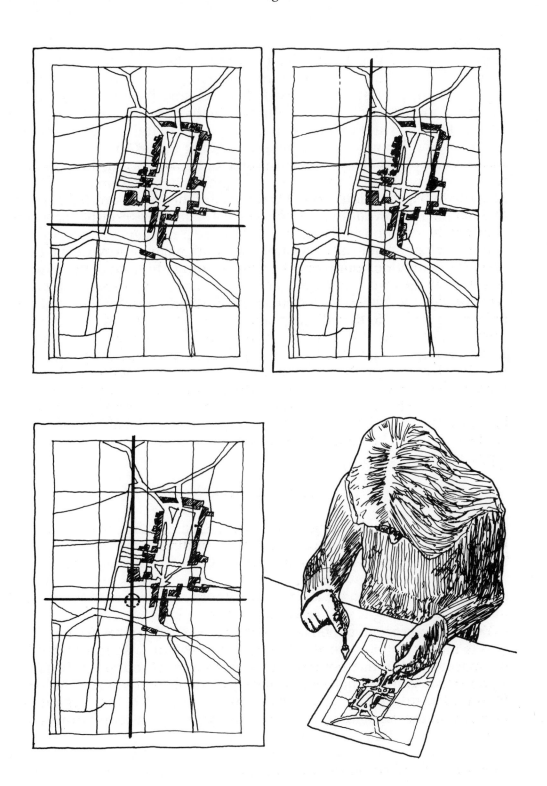

Figure 8.2: Map-dowsing: finding coordinates

your mind an image of your friend, or hold a sample of them (a lock of hair, perhaps) if you have one. First ask if they're in a place that's represented on the map (an Idiot response may mean No, or that they are confusing the issue somehow—do make sure they're willing to be 'watched' in this way!). Think about where they are *now*; try to build an image of it. You want to find the position. Point to the top-left corner of the map, and imagine a horizontal line going across the map: as you move your pointer slowly down the side of the map to the bottom- left corner, you want the pendulum to respond when that imaginary line passes over her position—in other words find her north-south coordinate. Do it. (How would you interpret No or Idiot responses, or more than one Yes response? Think about that for a moment). Once you've found just one north-south coordinate, do the same for the east-west coordinate, moving your pointer across the top or bottom of the map to sweep an imaginary vertical line across the map. Remember: you want your friend's position as it is *now*. Note down the results: check them with them later. How well did it work?

Results:

You'll now need your friend to keep some kind of diary of movements, because you're going to try to plot the various moves they've made through the day.

Exercise 101: Where were they?

At the end of the day, set up to repeat the last exercise. This time, though, you want to find the position your friend *was* in at each hour of the day. The rest of the exercise is exactly the same as before; but rather than using now as 'here in time', use the idea of 'now is other-when', an image-inary time. Start with 9.a.m.—imagine a clock showing 9.a.m., build an image of what *you* were doing at 9.a.m. this morning, and find her coordinates on the map *as if you were doing the dowsing at that time*, rather than now. (An Idiot response probably means she wasn't anywhere in the area represented by the map at that time.)

Repeat this for each hour of the day: 10 a.m., 11 a.m., and so on. Use your image of what you were doing at those times as a way of marking your point in time: but remember that you're looking for your friend at those times, not yourself! How well do your dowsing results compare with her notes?

Comments:

With practice, you'll find you can work out where someone's been—as long as you have their permission to do so. Some very strange and confusing things tend to happen if you don't—the Joker at work again, perhaps? And sometimes your 'wrong' results turn out to be more right than you think: one of my students found that she'd plotted out not where her friend was, but where she was *supposed* to be at that time (she'd been delayed)—which is very strange indeed . . . Still, what else would you expect when you put to use something that's entirely coincidence and mostly imaginary?

So let's stretch the coincidences a little further and try to plot out where your friend *will* be . . .

Exercise 102: Where will they be?

Once again, set up as for Exercise 100, but this time do it at the start of the day. Build an image of your friend as before: you're looking for *them*, the position as represented on this map. Start with *this* time as 'now' (which it is, of course): mark her position *now*. And now imagine the clock going round an hour: that point in the future is 'now', so mark her position as it is at this future 'now'. Repeat this for each hour of the day: imagine the clock going round, showing each future hour, and mark her position for each of those 'nows'. At the end of the day, compare notes again. How far into the future can you go? Can you get this to be as reliable as looking for where she is or where she was? If not, for what reason does it seem to go wrong?

Comments:

This set of exercises really does show up the paradoxes of time, something that we will, as promised, look at in Chapter 10. In time dowsing we're choosing and moving 'now'—our effective working point in time—much as we choose and move 'here' in other forms of dowsing. So it's easiest to work with when 'now' is the present, quite easy to work with a 'now' in the relatively recent past, fairly easy to work with the near future as long as what you're dealing with follows a fairly regular pattern (the good old 9-to-5 routine!), and not at all easy when the person you're tracking is *unpredictable*. Not surprising, really: that's the way that most things are, so don't expect dowsing to be any different!

Fixing the car

The popular image of dowsing is one that is definitely low-tech: the old water diviner with his wooden rod. But since the purpose of dowsing is simply to *find* things, whatever they are, we can also find uses for it in more modern technologies—some of them very hi-tech indeed.

For example, you can use dowsing to help you find and fix faults in your car. One of the most irritating types of fault is the kind that only happens intermittently. That's what happened to the tail-light on my motorcycle today: miles from home, the warning light came on, suggesting that the bulb was blown—and then it turned itself off. And flashed on again; then off; and so on for several miles. Then the warning stayed on for a while; then turned off, apparently when I used the front brake, and has stayed off ever since. And there was no obvious pattern: it didn't seem to be when I went over a bumpy stretch of road, or anything obvious like that. An intermittent fault: difficult to pin down, but it's there somewhere in the system.

Think back to a similar example from your own experience. Go back and remember how you traced it: sure, part of it would have been the usual logic of technology, but another part of it—without which you wouldn't have got anywhere—was just *letting* yourself see what was wrong. And that's where dowsing can help.

We've dowsed on maps. And a map is a representation of a place, a diagram or image of that place. So we can also dowse using other types of representations—for example, a schematic such as the wiring diagram for your car.

Exercise 103: Fault-finding

Imagine that there's a lighting fault on your car, like the tail-lamp flicker on my motorcycle that I described earlier. So open out the wiring schematic on the table. (If there actually *is* something wrong with your car, open out the respective diagram(s) for that part of the system in front of you instead.) Build in your mind an image of what you know is wrong with the system; not what you *think* is wrong, but the known symptoms of what you *know* is wrong. Imagine *being* in that system, being part of your car, with that fault happening within it, within 'you'. Using a pendulum in one hand, move a pointer around on the schematic, asking the pendulum to respond when the pointer is over the part of the diagram that represents the source of the fault—which may not necessarily be where you see the symptoms of the fault. (Alternatively, you could ask the pendulum, or miniature angle-rods, to point towards the representation of the source of the problem, leading you over the schematic as if it were a map of some actual place.) Do you get any *direct* sense of when your pointer is over the right place—a tingling in your fingers, for example?

Comments:

An Idiot response here would usually mean that you're looking on the wrong diagram: the problem isn't here, it's elsewhere in the total system. 'Un-ask the question', is what Idiot means: think wider. For example, there's no point in doing a detailed analysis of the carburettor if the fuel tank's empty . . . the pendulum can't do your thinking for you!

You can apply the same general technique to any kind of diagram or schematic. For instance, one friend used to dowse over electronic circuit diagrams to locate faults in his designs. He was so good at it that he eventually found he didn't need the pendulum at all: he could feel it directly in his fingers. Running his hands over the diagram, imagining himself being *in* the system and walking through its traces and components, he *knew* if the resistor or capacitor values were wrong—they would simply *feel* wrong. Direct knowing: merging his sensed knowledge of the image-inary world represented by the diagram with that of the 'real', tangible, everyday world.

Apply that same sense, that same overall awareness, to working on the diagrams for your car. And combine it with what we know of dowsing in time, to a different 'now', so that you can check for prospective problems *before* they happen.

Exercise 104: Preventive maintenance

Lay out all the diagrams of your car in front of you. Study them, build an image of them and of what they mean: imagine *being* the car. Ask yourself: What's the *next* part of the system that needs attention? What's the next component that will need replacing? Which of the fluid levels needs checking? Ask the pendulum (or whichever instrument you're using) to point you to that part of the system as represented by the diagrams; run a pointer over the diagrams, or let your instrument lead you there. Note down your results. Anything you hadn't expected?

Comments:

Do this on a regular basis for a while. Keep a detailed notebook of your results, then follow them up and compare your predictions with the physical reality. Get into the habit of looking at things from the *car's* point of view: do continue to do the conventional checks, of course, but learn this way to get it to tell you when it needs further attention before it becomes urgent.

In some ways dowsing is almost too analytical a tool for this. In learning to dowse, you've also been building up an ability to reach an overall sensing, an overall intuitive awareness—dowsing without instruments, dowsing without tools, dowsing just as you using you. Let's look at another way to do that last exercise.

Exercise 105: Look—no tools!

Lay the diagrams out in front of you again: but this time put down your dowsing tools, and close your eyes. Drop all thinking about what you'd expect needs looking at next; instead, just build up in your mind as detailed an image as you can of the car, as if looking at things from the car's point of view. Stand quietly, and ask your own inner knowing: Please show me what part of the car needs to be checked. Now, as you open your eyes: what do you see directly in front of you? Does any area stand out? What's the *first* section of any of the diagrams that you see? What does that tell you?

Results:

Just let yourself be drawn to look at particular places. Note what comes up in your mind as you do so. Just let go. Don't try: just let *it* tell *you*.

I realize that it isn't easy to let go: it goes counter to almost everything that we've been taught about 'common sense'. We've had so much practice at talking at things that it's hard to listen! But just try it: practise it. Remember the Fool's Law: things can work if you let them—especially if you let them work in unexpected ways. And while this may seem very unexpected, it *does* work: it's just another form of dowsing, after all. Entirely co-incidence, mostly image-inary: being put to practical use.

9.

The Greater Toolkit

Dowsing is not an end in itself. It's a useful *part* of our toolkit: not the whole thing. In learning about dowsing we also need to learn how to use it in conjunction with some of our other ways of working in the world, our other ways of putting coincidence to use. Our aim now, as we move towards the end of the book, should be to understand not just where dowsing fits in the toolkit of ideas and approaches for dealing with the world, but also where the whole toolkit fits in that context, too. It's important that we don't allow ourselves to get stuck on dowsing alone: think wider, and *be* wider in your awareness!

Getting unstuck

There's an infamous state, when something doesn't work and we don't know what to do: we call it 'being stuck'. It's not a pleasant state to be in. Since much of my own work is research or analysis, I'm all too familiar with that state . . .

Dowsing, on its own, is not the best of tools for dealing with that situation. If you ask it 'What do I do now?', you'll probably get an answer of Yes. Or Idiot, of course. Which is not exactly helpful.

So we have to look elsewhere for ideas. And if we can actually manage to sit quietly for a while, without giving in to the panic—in other words, just let ourselves 'do no-thing'—we'll usually find that ideas do arise. A few of those ideas will be good, or at least lead on to something that's useful; but most of them will be just plain rubbish. So how do we separate the good from the bad?

That's the point where your dowsing comes in. It can't generate new ideas for you: but it can help you test them. Here's one exercise—best done with a pendulum—that you could try:

Exercise 106: Let the ideas flow . . .

You'll need to keep your writing hand free for this one, so practise using the pendulum in your other hand for a while if necessary. Then sit quietly with a pencil, a pad and a pendulum, and just let the ideas flow. Swing the pendulum gently in Neutral. Keep your subject area in mind: just see what arises. And watch, with the corner of your eye, the pendulum's response to each. If you get any kind of clear response—whether Yes, No or Idiot—write a brief note to yourself about the idea and the pendulum's response to it, and then return to your musings and meditations. Continue doing this for a while—half an hour, perhaps. Then stop, and look more closely at what you've written down: note the pendulum's responses to that as you do so. Take one of those ideas, frame it as the main idea at the forefront of your mind, and repeat the whole sequence once more—and perhaps for each of those ideas in that first list. Where does this procedure take you?

Comments:

What we're doing here is using the pendulum as a background support to what is, in effect, a ritual. (There's nothing odd in this: every technology has its rituals, which are mainly used to re-emphasize awareness, and especially to make visible what *isn't* there—my favourite example is the pilot's pre-take-off check, that long, almost chanted, check list, making sure that everything is as it should be before rolling down the runway.) Thinking too hard only gets in the way when we're stuck: so we're using the pendulum's quiet, almost hypnotic, background movement to help us to maintain a state of 'not-thinking', so that new ideas can come through.

It works: mainly by not doing anything at all. Or, more to the point, by 'doing no-thing' and letting other aspects of your mind work with the Fool's Law, to help get you unstuck. Use it: but don't *try*, of course!

Very often we need much the same kind of unstuckness when trying to find out about something in the library. Despite all those librarians' tools of card-indexes and the rest, trying too hard often just makes it harder—just as it does with trying to fix the car. With the help of the conventional tools, you've tried the obvious books—page by page, probably—and you haven't found what you need. You know the information's in there *somewhere*: but where? So once again we can use our knowledge of dowsing and of the Fool's Law to help us.

Exercise 107: A fact-finding tour

You need to find a particular piece of information about something. Frame in your mind, as clearly as you can, the general area of what you're looking for, but *without* being too specific—you need to leave the Fool's Law some space to play within. Frame in your mind also that you want your dowsing to lead you to something that can tell you more about your enquiry. So use a pendulum, or perhaps one of the 'invisible' techniques, and walk past the aisles of books, asking your dowsing which aisle to look into in more detail. Assuming it selects just one aisle, go down it, to get your dowsing to pick out an area, a shelf, a book. And see what you've got. You may be lucky, and hit it right first time: but often the Joker likes playing games with us in this kind of hunt, so don't worry if the book seems at first to be irrelevant. To make sense of it, apply the crazy logic of the Fool's Law, and allow it to be right in an *unexpected* way. What does it suggest to you? What ideas arise? Apply the idea-testing techniques of the last exercise (Exercise 106): where do they lead you? At each stage, follow these new leads: you'll be surprised at what you find out! Also, as with the previous exercise, re-frame your enquiry as necessary, refining your quest, making several passes through the library. Do you get the information you need? What else do you find? Is this quicker than a page-by-page search of every 'appropriate' item in the library?

_____

Comments:

_____

To get this to work well you need to develop an ability to let go, to play, to indulge in what seems like childish games. Don't worry if you feel foolish: that's one reason why it's called the Fool's Law!

It all looks random, perhaps: but in fact it has a subtle order to it. What you're doing is using your dowsing to engage a badly under-used aspect of the mind, a kind of 'pattern-matcher' sense that sees connections between bits and pieces of information that we see or remember. We experience this sense most often in dreaming—and, as in dreams, the way it labels connections can sometimes seem very strange indeed. Visual puns, alliterations, things out of place, and every other form of bad joke, they're all there: but what else would you expect from the Joker?

So play him at his own game: be a Joker too. Read the book upside down; read every third letter; or the first and last word on every page. Let there be enough 'noise', and the signal you need will eventually filter through: if you apply the filters too early, by trying to control the process or force it to make sense in the way that you expect, you're likely to shut *everything* out. So give your imagination free rein: let that 'pattern-matcher' side of your mind lead you, through its strange but merry dances, to the information you need. Play! It's fun: enjoy it! That's the whole idea of learning a new skill, surely?

The diviner's toolkit

When you're looking for a way to get unstuck, sometimes the best way of working—especially when you're more concerned with context than content—is to use something that has a rich visual symbolism. And here we wander onto another set of tools that are even older than dowsing: those many different 'pattern-reading' techniques that have been used since time immemorial for *divining* meaning from all manner of coincidences. Many of them have a '-mancy' ending: cartomancy, geomancy—even dowsing was known as 'rhabdomancy' at one time.

But to start with, one easy source of a rich symbolism is your own dreams. With a little practice it's quite easy, and certainly instructive, to keep a record of your dreams. For most people they can disappear from memory within minutes, or even seconds, after waking if they're not written down straight away: so keep a pad beside your bed, and get them down onto paper as soon as you're awake enough to hold a pencil. Do this for about a week, until you've a good pile of material to work with.

It won't take you long, reading through, to see where some of the images come from. A lot of dreaming is similar to what's called 'garbage collection' in computing: shuffling prominent ideas and images of the previous day with those of months ago, all being moved into a kind of long-term storage area. But it seems those ideas are stored with some kind of associative 'handle', so that we can get at them in future—and it's in those associations that the Joker gets to play some of his strangest games.

Some of those connections, those 'handles', are bizarre: puns, things out of place, alliterations, all that stuff again. There are themes within dreams that run for weeks, and then just stop. It often seems that there's no way you can make sense of dreams. And that's probably true if you're looking for direct sense. But although it mostly *is* nonsense, it's nonsense with a quite separate but *indirect* idea of order surrounding it. The 'handles' are built by the pattern-matching part of the mind, so watch for patterns, however obscure. And this is where your dowsing can help you, of course: use your written-down dreams as the source-material for the 'free flow' exercise (Exercise 106), that we looked at earlier in this chapter.

Don't be too quick to ignore dreams: with practice, they can be very useful indeed. One friend, a professional programmer, makes a habit of studying the text of a program problem until well into the night, and then quite literally 'sleeps on it': trying hard, thinking hard, and then quite deliberately letting go into the freer world of dreams—another variant on 'thinking narrow, being wide'. He finds that, somewhere within his dream, there'll be a peculiar juxtaposition, something appearing out of place, which he can then play with as a clue to tell him where to look in his work the next day. Sometimes he uses a pendulum to help him work it out; sometimes that other sense behind dowsing comes into play, without needing the pendulum 'ritual' to help it along. The technique works well for him, and for others too—see how well you can get it to work for you!

One of the advantages of using the symbolism of dreams is also one of its disadvantages: it's all yours, so in some ways you're the only one who could make sense of it. Sometimes it's a lot easier to use a set of symbols that's 'pre-packaged', so to speak, so that you can use someone else's ideas to help you interpret it. This is especially true if you're facing a question such as 'What do I do now?', for which your dowsing on its own isn't going to be much use. So this is where tools like the Tarot can come in handy . . . especially if you combine them with your dowsing.

For the next exercise you'll need a Tarot pack, along with some kind of description of usual interpretations for the cards. There are a bewildering variety of decks and books available at the moment but you choose: as with your dowsing instruments, what works best is whatever works best for *you*.

The layout and order of the cards in Figure 9.1 is probably the oldest, and certainly the best-known 'spread'. It's certainly a good one for a general 'What's the context . . . ?' kind of question.

It's important to realize that these tools aren't actually much good at *content*—'You'll meet a tall dark stranger . . .' and all that stuff. What they are good at is *context*: the background, a general set of suggestions for how to interpret the coincidences going on around you. So we can combine the usual summaries with the kind of 'flow of ideas' dowsing work we were doing back in Exercise 106, to get an easier way of making sense of the symbolism and imagery that arises.

Figure 9.1: 'Celtic Cross' tarot spread

Exercise 108: The noble art of cartomancy

Frame in your mind an issue that's been concerning you—describe it to yourself much as you've been doing with your dowsing. Shuffle the Tarot pack a few times, keeping your issue in mind as you do so. Lay out 10 cards, face up, in the order shown in Figure 9.1. Note the shorthand entry for each card in the list in Table 9.1 as you do so: for the first card, note to yourself 'This is what is Underlying this matter', 'This is what is Current in this matter' for the second, and so on for each of the cards. Continue until the spread is complete. Wait for a moment. Then open your Tarot book at the entry which describes the card you now have in the Underlying place (the first card in the sequence). As you read through the text, use your dowsing (probably a pendulum or a finger-rubbing technique) to help you pick out passages which seem particularly relevant in the context of (for this card) matters past, of underlying, and so on. Do the same for the other nine cards,

Table 9.1: Sequence and context for Celtic Cross spread

1	*Underlying*	Concerns now in the past (esp. emotional)
2	*Current*	Concerns now in the present (esp. emotional)
3	*Above*	Concerns in conscious awareness; hopes, issues, desires in general
4	*Below*	Concerns in subconscious, or hopes and desires not in conscious awareness
5	*Inward*	Inward to self: work, creativity, obstacles—ability to use coincidences
6	*Outward*	Outward from self: especially decision-making, courage to take responsibility
7	*Effects*	Possible results on work, creativity, outer world
8	*Relationships*	Impact on friends, family, partners in any sense
9	*Hopes or fears*	Impact on personal growth and similar issues, concerns of past or future
10	*Expression*	Context expressed from inner nature, or released from inner nature

reading the text for each in its context as described in Table 9.1, with your dowsing emphasizing parts of the text as in the 'free-flow' exercise (Exercise 106). In what ways does this help you to make the context of your issue more clear or easy to understand?

Comments:

Sometimes it's useful to compare several different Tarot books at once, using your dowsing to pick out the most relevant passages for each card, regardless of the source of the interpretation.

I've also found this technique helpful for interpreting the *I Ching*, which usually has a number of possible interpretations for each line in a given hexagram. You can also use your dowsing to build the hexagram itself.

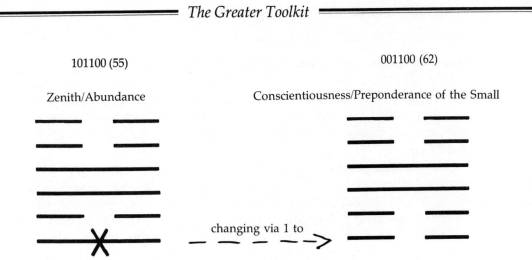

101100 (55)   001100 (62)

Zenith/Abundance   Conscientiousness/Preponderance of the Small

changing via 1 to

Figure 9.2: An example 'I Ching' hexagram

Exercise 109: Casting the Oracle

As with the Tarot exercise above, frame in your mind an issue that's been concerning you: but this time frame it rather more definitely as a question asking about the context surrounding that issue, the way to approach that issue. With this question in mind, you now want to use your dowsing to build a hexagram, a pattern of six lines, starting with the lowest line. For each line (still keeping your main quest in mind), ask two questions: 'Is this line firm?' (a No means 'broken') and 'Is this line fixed?' (a No means 'moving'). Mark the line according to the results (see Figure 9.2), and repeat until you've built the complete six-line hexagram. This describes the context of your issue in the present or near-future. If any of the lines are 'moving', make a copy of the pattern, but with any moving lines changed to their opposite—firm to broken, broken to firm (again, see the example in Figure 9.2): the resultant new hexagram is what the initial context will change to over a period of time. Use the 'free-flow' technique (Exercise 106 again) to get your dowsing to emphasize particular passages of the text, as in the interpretation for this hexagram (or hexagrams) in one of the many translations of the *I Ching*. What are the results?

Comments:

We can, of course, go from one extreme to another, and go from the rigid formality and structure of the *I Ching* to the much more open and indeterminate subtleties of geomancy—sensing the currents of the earth itself. Here we have no 'pre-packaged' interpretation of coincidences, but are pushed instead towards making our own sense of what we find.

We've already started with this, looking at water divining: we recognized then that what we perceived as 'water lines' was, in essence, a way of describing flows and currents beneath the surface. The picture became more complicated with that knot-like pattern that occurs when two or more water lines cross each other—the water probably doesn't move in that 'knot' pattern, but that's how we perceive it. It's perhaps best understood as a kind of interaction of energies and perceptions, partly real (in the sense of physical-ness), and partly image-inary.

Exercise 110: The subtle art of geomancy

Go out into the country somewhere, preferably to some place that would have been thought of as 'sacred' in older times: a well, a quiet grove of trees, an ancient crossroads, perhaps even a small stone circle. Sit there quietly for a while. Now use your dowsing to trace the paths of water lines: you're looking for the patterns of underground water. What shapes do they plot out? Next, look for patterns that are similar, but are at the surface rather than below: what differences can you see? What is the difference in *feel* between these two types of patterns? Finally, see if you can find any patterns from some kind of natural energies (undefined—rather as we 'un-defined' auras earlier) that are *above* ground—between ground level and perhaps 20 feet up. Once again, what differences can you see? What is the difference in *feel* between these new patterns of image-inary energies, and the previous ones? And can you sense an overall kind of pattern, linking these three different levels into one single web or network?

Results:

For many years the type of dowsing involved in that last exercise was my major interest. In fact one of the reasons I started teaching dowsing was that I needed people who could check my research results. So I worked, with many others, on a long series of studies of all manner of sacred and not-so-sacred sites throughout the British Isles, such as the stone circle at Rollright in Oxfordshire, 4,000 or more years old, and source of many legends and folk-tales. And we found that sometimes the energies were more than just image-inary: there are anomalies in several different types of physical energies too—micro-magnetic, microwave, ultrasonic, even distortions in cosmic radiation patterns. (You'll find more detail on this in some of the books listed in the Appendix, including my own *Needles of Stone*.)

Figure 9.3: Rollright stone circle, Oxfordshire

There are any number of systems of geomancy, systems that describe these and many other patterns and try to put them to use in a practical way. The ancient Chinese system, *Feng Shui* (literally 'wind-water') is just one example; the modern concept of 'archaeo-astronomy', which describes sites in terms of astronomical alignment, is another. Other theories note the geometry of the sites; yet others look at patterns on a larger scale, making up what seem to be landscape zodiacs. And so it goes on.

And on, and on: there's no end to it. There never is an end to it. The closer you look, the more you analyse, the more detail there is to find; and the more detail there is, the more patterns there are to find. In fact, it all sounds suspiciously like the Joker at work . . .

Dowsing is just another tool in the analytical toolkit. And this is one of those times when the toolkit itself can get in the way of our understanding of what's going on. So, for a while, let's just forget the toolkit, and move beyond analysis, beyond the toolkit, into a wider awareness.

Beyond the toolkit

Working with dowsing tools, you're always looking, always asking questions, and expecting Reality Department to come up with some sensible answer. It's a good way of working: it produces results, in fact almost all of the modern world has come out of that approach. But sometimes, just sometimes, it's better to stop trying, stop talking, and simply to *listen*.

Exercise 111: Finding your place

Go back to the place you visited for the last exercise (Exercise 110), and use your dowsing for a while, in the same way you did then. Notice if there are any changes in the patterns since your last visit; and while you're working let that awareness that you use in dowsing, of 'thinking narrow, being wide' move your sensing wide and open. After a while, stop dowsing. And just listen to the place; don't try, just put down your dowsing tools and sit quietly for a while. Still quiet, stand up, look around you. And move, as the whim takes you, to places that seem interesting—for no definite reason, but just *interesting*. By 'doing no-thing', find your *own* place, your own places within this space. Note how you feel at each of these points: listen to your inner senses, how your body and your mind and your emotions respond to the changes in the environment. What do you sense, what do you learn? Do you find it hard to 'do no-thing'?

Comments:

It's not easy to 'do no-thing': it's against all of our training. The fact is, it works. Very often the best tool is no tool at all. Just you using you: nothing else.

It's all coincidence, you could say: entirely co-incidence, mostly image-inary. But then *everything* is. The whole point is to find a way to put it to practical use, in learning to recognize when some co-incidence is useful. Or, as in this case, simply feels *right*.

So now we've come full circle. We started off without the dowsing tools; now we've come to a place where, in some ways, you no longer need them. You've gone beyond them. Or are beginning to do so, at any rate.

In learning to use the tools, you've begun to learn more and more about how you *know*. Beyond any system, beyond any rules: knowing, without question, what you know—and also what you don't know. In the end, the knowing is all there is: and that knowing *is* you.

That's not easy. It really is a skill: one that certainly will take you a lifetime's practice to master. So don't hurry: just take your time, just allow yourself to learn it, observing and understanding your own ways of interacting with the world. And in the meantime, your dowsing skills are there to help you, as and when you need them. They're all yours: use them well!

10.

So How Does Dowsing Work?

I did promise that we'd look at how dowsing works, how it all happens. But perhaps the best way to start this section is for you to ask yourself the same question:

Exercise 112: So how does dowsing work?

Ignore the advice of any supposed 'authorities' (including mine). Look back at what you've learned from your *own* experience, developing your own dowsing skills. Assuming that you're satisfied that it does work—for others, if not as yet for yourself—have you formed any clear ideas about how it all works? (A clue: if you're certain you know how it all works, you're probably not looking close enough . . .)

_____

Comments:

_____

I'll be honest: I don't know how it works either. At least I *know* that I don't know, which is something. Every time I try to pin it down to a particular theory, a particular approach, it always manages to wriggle around and present me with something that works in a way that I didn't expect. As long as I've *let* it work, of course.

Dowsing has always done this. Look at some research reports—Tromp in the '30s, Maby and Franklin in the '40s, Taylor in the '70s—and you'll see the same pattern every time. Whenever someone's tried to do a scientific study, whatever makes dowsing work has either sulked and refused to play at all in the laboratory (though continued to work quite happily outside), or followed the experimenter's theory for a while and then suddenly changed its mind, and worked some other way instead. Awkward as ever!

But in a way there's no point. As we've seen, we don't really *need* to know how it all works, as long as it does actually work. Dowsing is far more a technology than a science: and all we need to know in any technology is how it can be *worked*. Any theories we might have are—or should be—just sources of ideas for better ways to work it in practice.

It might be much more comfortable to have an explanation that looks something like what other people would accept as 'fact': but we don't have one. None that would stand up to any real scrutiny, anyway. Still, the one fact that we *do* have is that it does work, for most people—with a little practice and a few interesting acts of mental acrobatics, perhaps—but it *does* work. (Assuming that you have bothered to do at least some of the exercises by now, you'll have proved that to yourself in practice.) So even without an explanation, it still works!

And that's why I've been careful, throughout this book, to explain the whole process by not explaining it at all, with that simple 'non-explanation' that it's all co-incidence and mostly image-inary. We're putting coincidence to practical use. Without some consistent theory that truly could encompass every aspect of dowsing, that really *is* all we can say about it.

But if that's so, what is coincidence?

It's all co-incidence

The question is more important than it looks. At first, the answer seems to be obvious: it's just coincidence, isn't it? There doesn't seem to be any point to the question. But stop for a moment, and try to describe it in relation to anything else: and you'll find you can't. Coincidence is, well, you know: *coincidence*.

All we can do is describe it as itself. We can use an alternate name—'event', for example—but since that is exactly the same, that tells us nothing. And yet it's very real: we certainly experience it. So what *is* it?

In one sense coincidences don't have meaning: they're just events. But in another sense they most certainly *do* have meaning: a peculiar thread that cuts across all our ideas about what is and isn't 'normal' in our lives. For most of what we experience, we have a good idea of what supposedly caused what: but we also all have many examples of events and connections—very real connections—that make no sense at all in terms of cause and effect. There is a kind of sense there, but just *what* is not at all easy to grasp.

Exercise 113: When is coincidence more than coincidence?

Look back in your memory, and remember events that stand out because of their strangeness: for example, climbing a mountain and finding a colleague from 10 years ago waiting at the top. Take a few examples of your own, and ask yourself: Why do they stand out? What is that sense of 'meaningfulness' in what is often an otherwise meaningless event? What, for you, made these coincidences more than 'mere coincidences'?

Comments:

One thing that makes these events seem so strange is that they're out of our control. Cause-and-effect we understand; these games of the Joker we don't. They're even a little frightening at times—perhaps because our sense of security, in this culture, comes from our relative certainty of being able to predict what's going to happen.

But given the infinite nature of reality and our finite grasp of events, the best we can do with causality is predict what's *likely* to happen, and even then only in the crudest physical terms. Since we've all been told endlessly since childhood that things happen because this causes that (and so on), it's a bit of a surprise when we finally realize just how limited in usefulness—as a *predictive* tool—the concept of causality can be:

Exercise 114: . . . and what caused that?

Just ask yourself: what caused you to be reading this book? And what were the causes that led you to that cause? Could you have predicted that those 'first' causes—let alone the infinite others before them, such as those that led *me* to be writing this book—would have led you to be reading *this* word, now?

Comments:

Look at it like that, and it's obvious that there's something else. Just what that 'something else' actually happens to be is not really something we can grasp: as with time—another 'something' that is real yet quite intangible—it just *is*, and that's about all we can say.

Whenever we think of cause and effect, we're thinking in terms of *time*. Whatever event we describe as the 'cause' always occurs *before* its supposed 'effect'. In other words cause-effect chains are patterns in time. And precisely because they *are* patterns that we can recognize, we can use them in a predictive way (though often we can perceive them as recognizable patterns only *after* they've occurred, which may be a little late . . .). We don't actually know *why* they are patterns, without describing reasons 'why' in terms of others of those same patterns—a classic example of circular reasoning which gets us nowhere. So that's all they are: patterns.

They're not the only ones: there are also these other patterns, such as the ones we've been studying and learning to recognize in this book, that seem to occur 'acausally', quite outside of time. Some of them, clusterings of apparently random events, Kammerer termed 'serialities'; others, groups of entities (concepts, physical events, dream images and the like) occurring at the same moment and linked by a *subjective* sense of meaning, were termed 'synchronicities' by Carl Jung. But there are many other classes of these acausal connections: and at least one of them, it seems to me, is what is behind dowsing. An understanding of causality may be the key to the conventional technologies: but an understanding of acausality, these connections without connections, leads us to the equally real technology of dowsing, and much more besides.

So we never will be able to describe what causes dowsing to work, because whatever makes it do so, whatever it is that's behind it, exists largely outside of any concept of cause and effect. It seems increasingly likely that the only truthful answer to the question 'What makes dowsing work?' is 'Yes'. Or 'Idiot', perhaps—un-ask the question'.

The Norse legends described life as a web, a roll of cloth being woven by the three Fates, the 'three sisters of wyrd'. So, by analogy, causality is the weft of that web, threaded across time; and acausality is the cross-warp, weaving its multi-coloured way through the normality of our lives. And coincidences? They're the knots in the mesh, the points where the threads co-incide and cross. Coincidences are points that exist not just in time and space, but also quite outside them, totally beyond those limitations, in fact cutting *across* anything we could understand as time or space.

So everything really is all coincidence: it's up to us whether we put those coincidences, those opportunities, to use. Dowsing is entirely co-incidence, mostly image-inary: using our imagination to put coincidences to use. In choosing to do so we also choose to move across that warp, moving momentarily outside time and space—and, perhaps, change our fates in the process!

A question of time

I did also promise, earlier in the book, that we'd take a look at time, and especially why dowsing in time is so fraught with difficulties.

If you've managed to make sense of the discussion above, you'll see that the reason is quite simple—even if the implications are anything but simple! Our experience of events is of coincidences in a web of causality and acausality, in which time is in some ways a dimension. We see cause-and-effect as recognizable patterns of events in a sequence in time. And we can also see other patterns, and learn to recognize other acausal patterns that run *across* the apparent linearity of time—and those, it seems, are what we're working with when we're dowsing in time.

What confuses everything is that while we *experience* time, it's quite imaginary. The past is gone, the future never here: all we can ever know for certain is *now*—a 'now' that we can never grasp, because as soon as we observe it, it's ceased to be the same 'now'. So time doesn't exist—at least, not in the sense that would apply to those three tangible dimensions of height, width and depth.

All physical events, the effects of causes, are patterns in time—and since we see them as patterns *in* time, it makes it very difficult to look at time itself. The physical definition of our standard unit of time, the second, is described in terms of the duration of a specific frequency of radio waves: another example of circular reasoning, since frequency is itself defined in terms of time. And time is assumed to be linear and regular, an assumption which we have no way to check at all, since any method for doing so would exist within that same time, linear or non-linear, regular or irregular.

Physical time is assumed to be linear (relativity theory notwithstanding). But those cross-currents of coincidence are more like loops, threading back and forth through our lives. In dowsing, we're linking across acausal loops in time and space in a way that we can still barely comprehend.

Our experience of time is anything but linear: 10 minutes of rushing to catch a train is a far shorter period of time than 10 minutes waiting for it at the other end. And for tribal people, time is measured by the day, or the season, and the shortest recognized time-unit may well be the time a pot takes to boil—which, as we all know, is far longer if you watch it than if you don't.

Time is imaginary. And coincidences are events both within time and outside of it—some of them points where the Joker's warped mind cuts across the threads of normality, giving us those chaotically confusing but useful coincidences I call 'Normal Rules'. It's all entirely coincidence, mostly imaginary.

The past is imaginary: a photograph, as a record of a moment in time, is literally 'image-inary'. And the future is imaginary: we can only imagine it, because it doesn't yet exist in any tangible sense. We push towards our choice of future with intention, or will. But since everybody else is doing the same, there's no way we can predict the outcome with any certainty. We can see when something is *likely* to happen: but there's no way that we can ever be certain that that particular image-inary world will ever coincide exactly with the physical world at the precise moment we'd need for certainty. There are just too many forces acting upon it, too many threads of time pulling the future this way and that.

Whichever way we look at it, time is a maze of paradoxes.

So, given the paradoxical nature of time, the best we can ever hope to achieve, in dowsing with a different 'now', is a past or future with a high *probability* of being valid. The conventional tool of statistics won't help us much, either: statistics are only useful with large numbers of events, whereas here we're looking at just one. All you're left with, in the end, is your skill at interpreting possibilities. And that, in effect, is what you've been learning and practising in this book.

So what does it all mean? What *is* time? In a way, it's probably best to use another 'non-explanation', and say that it just *is*: whatever it means, we'll find out later with all the advantages of hindsight.

With both time and coincidence, we seem to end up going round in circles if we try to make sense of them in a way that we can describe in 'objective' terms to others. They just *are*: that's all. But we *can* put them both to practical use, as long as we can accept that we'll probably only understand them in our own experience and practice.

If you look at it in that way, getting those coincidences of your dowsing to work well for you is also a question of time: a matter of taking the time to put it into practice. Doing it: not talking about it, or thinking about it, or arguing about it, but *doing it*.

Since practice is really what matters, that's probably the best way to end this book. And that's why the next (and final) chapter contains nothing but practice!

11.

A Test of Skill

We've now come to the end of all I can show you here: the rest is up to you, to put what you've learnt here into practical experience. To get you started on this next stage, here are a few suggestions of things on which to try out your dowsing.

The real world

For a start, apply your new knowledge to your routine dealings with the real world.

One obvious place to begin is where we first started, looking for pipes and the like. Next time you or a friend have some kind of trouble with a pipe or a cable, use your dowsing to look for it before resorting to conventional methods or tools such as a metal detector.

The point here is that you won't have to rely on your dowsing—if you don't get it right, you *can* find it by conventional methods if you have to. But it will give you some real dowsing practice in a real-world situation. And in many ways your dowsing, even at this stage, could well be more reliable than the kind of 'metal detector' that's used to find plastic water pipes—especially if the pipe is buried several feet deep, as they often are.

We went through the principles of how to deal with this in Exercise 69, back in Chapter 6. First decide on some way to image what you're looking for: a sample, a drawing, some kind of clear description to yourself, or whatever. Make it clear in your mind what you're looking for: *this* pipe, or *this* cable. Go to some point along it where it reaches the surface: you want to be following *this* pipe, *this* cable. *This* is what I'm looking for.

Assume for now that you'll be looking for a leak in a water pipe. (The principles for finding a crack in a cable are exactly the same—just change the wording a little!) So, choose your instrument, and first plot out the route of the pipe. Try it two ways: first crossing and recrossing what you believe is the route, building up a pattern of point-responses that you could link together in what should be the path of the pipe; and start from some known place, and 'ride' the pipe, using the instrument's directional responses to show you which way to go. If you're using angle rods, notice how you can let them 'squint'—angle slightly towards each other—as you ride the path: there's a definite 'flat' or 'nothingness' feel, with the rods going back to the parallel Neutral, if you miss your direction along the route.

Watch out too for any 'this is different' responses: angle rods opening out instead of pointing slightly inward, or the pendulum coming to a dead stop, or whatever. This kind of reaction may be the point of the break, although we're not yet specifically looking for it.

Once you're reasonably comfortable about the route, go back to the start and walk along it again, this time with the idea in mind of 'Give me a response when I'm over the break (or a break) in this pipe'. Don't stop at the first break you find: there may, unfortunately, be several breaks, so remember to check the entire length of the pipe that you need to inspect.

When you've done that, recheck your work, going right back to the beginning. Clear your mind of the previous test, tell yourself you've never been here before, and start again. Compare the results: if there are differences—which, even at this stage, is not at all unlikely—look back in your memory at what you *felt* at those points of difference during each of the two passes. There is a real clarity of feeling about dowsing when it's right, just as you *know* when you've hit the ball well—or badly—with a tennis racket. Go with those feelings: they're usually right.

If necessary, go over your work a third time, but don't retry and retry and retry: that usually makes things worse. Just let yourself find it.

And now, of course, the real test: physical proof. If you have some conventional tool such as a metal detector (if appropriate) to compare your dowsing with, use it. Or perhaps try the water-engineer's 'listening pole'—a wooden rod with one end resting on the ground and the other against the ear, to listen for the sound of water moving out of the break: with practice, as with dowsing, it's a surprisingly sensitive tool. Check everything: see if you get the same results as with your dowsing.

Then dig, at the places you've selected. If you'd picked out different places with different tools, which one (if either!) was right? How accurate was your dowsing?

Don't be upset if, even now, your dowsing seems completely wrong. Remember that you are still only learning: this is supposed to be a practice piece, not a final examination! And you wouldn't be the first one to get things wrong: the first time I did this exercise for real, I too made a complete fool of myself in front of the local plumber... But the next time I tried it, looking for a cracked drainpipe on a nearby farm, I really surprised the builder who'd come to mend it—and, I'll admit, surprised myself as well—by picking out the exact spot of the break to within a matter of inches, in half-frozen, muddy ground with icy water everywhere. So it does work: when you can let it. And that part of the skill really *does* take practice.

The advantage of practising your dowsing on this kind of work is that if you get it wrong, it doesn't matter much: it's cost you no more than a matter of minutes to try it. And if you *do* get it right—or even nearly right, close enough to work out by observation what to do next—you'll have saved that small expenditure of time many times over. In any case, almost *anything* is better than having to resort to the old 'brute force and ignorance' method of digging up the entire length of the pipe!

It is important, though, not to have to *rely* on your dowsing results: you're still at too early a stage to be able to take that risk with a high degree of certainty. Things do go wrong: accept it, learn from each so-called mistake, and you'll get on much quicker. And watch for the Joker's games, too… Especially, *don't* rely on your dowsing alone if you're looking for power-cables: it's just too dangerous. So *do* check your results with conventional tools: if you're looking for cables inside a house wall, for example, you could check with one of the small household-type metal detectors that are purpose-built for that job.

Do the dowsing first, then check with physical tools. Make a habit of using your dowsing whenever you can in this kind of work. Learn to watch for the *feelings* that tell you when you're on track and when you're not. And through that observation of yourself as you work, you'll learn to make better connections between the image-inary worlds of your dowsing and physical reality—learning to work ever more reliably in the real world.

Party games

If you go back through the exercises you've done in this book, you'll find plenty of other ways in which you can apply your dowsing in the real world: finding your keys, for example, as we also looked at in Chapter 6. You can also try out a whole series of parlour games, such as 'hunt the thimble' and the like.

The advantage of using parlour games as dowsing exercises is that they always involve more than one person. As long as everyone is willing to play along—with the emphasis on *play*—then you'll all be able to encourage each other to improve, with far less risk of getting stuck in some minor doubt or difficulty. The trick here is to get into the habit of balancing seriousness—'I need to get this *right*!'—with light-heartedness: learn to meet the Joker on his own ground, and you'll see a marked improvement in the reliability of your results.

So just play for a while. Take turns at childish games. 'Hunt the thimble': hide something small like a thimble or a nut under one of three cups, and use your dowsing to find out which one it's under. Sort a pack of playing cards into black and red, into suits, into royalty or number cards, or any which way you fancy. Use the usual question-and-answer dowsing routines to find out each others' minor personal details, such as body weight or birthday.

And so on: there are plenty of others to choose from. Just cast your mind back to your childhood and you'll remember several more to play with. Don't try: you don't need to try, so don't bother. You don't need to compete, either: encourage each other instead. Remember your childish innocence when you first played these games: rebuild that state of mind, and just let yourself let things work.

Try doing the same games both with actual dowsing tools and with some of the 'invisible' dowsing techniques. Then try blind guesswork: find out what difference it makes if you choose quickly or think long and hard. Try the games blindfold, so that you *have* to rely on a wider sense and awareness. Try them with your friends mentally encouraging you, or ignoring you, or sending confusing signals, or chattering and creating as much disturbance as possible. Experiment: observe the differences. That's the best way to learn.

Another exercise that's fun with a group of people is what I call 'paperless paper chase'. It's a variant on 'hide and seek', the difference being that you not only have to find the person who's hiding, but also to find the path they took while going to hide. What makes it even more interesting, from a dowsing point of view, is that if there are several people all running around the place using dowsing to try to find someone, they tend to leave their own imaginary trails behind them—which can really add to the confusion if you don't take a great deal of care!

So go out to a wood or a park. Select one of your group to act as the 'hare' that the rest of you intend to find. Choose a time limit—half an hour, say—in which you've got to find the 'hare': arrange to all meet up at a known place after that. And let the 'hare' go off to hide.

Now begin your search for the 'hare'. Decide whether you're going to search as a group or as individuals—if the latter, you're best to go off at intervals rather than all at the same time. Each of you build an image of the 'hare', or get them to leave behind, before they go off to hide, something that you can each use as a sample to find them with.

You know that they started from the same place as you, so you do know at least one point on their trail. Follow it, using directional dowsing techniques. Remember that you're trying to plot the path they took as well as where they're in hiding, so take care not to be misled by false trails and loop-backs that they may have done to confuse you. And, especially if you're doing this individually, take great care to keep the image of *them*—the 'hare'—in mind at all times: don't get sidetracked either by other people's trails or other people's expectations of their trail. Keep your mind on your own work: play with it, and just let the answers arise.

At the end, compare notes, and try again. If it's your turn to be the 'hare' experiment to see what difference (if any) your attitude makes when you lay the trail for the others to follow: at one time pay attention to the idea that you're laying a trail, and at another time occupy your mind with background chatter so that you don't have time to think of anything much at all. As with the other games, observe how these things work with you and with others: and in observing, learn from what you discover.

It's a game, a pleasant diversion for an afternoon or two. If the use isn't obvious now, don't worry: you will in time find yourself finding other uses for these skills, in every aspect of everyday life. Since it's all co-incidence anyway, you may as well put it to use, and enjoy yourself in the process!

A real test of skill

To complete this workbook, we have a real test of your new skills for you to try—and if you succeed, you could reasonably consider it to be your 'masterpiece' as a dowser.

Below are two sketch-maps: one of the Glastonbury area of Somerset in England, the other of part of the Marin peninsula, north of San Francisco in California. *Somewhere* in the public lands in each of those two areas is a target for you to find by dowsing: a brass medallion on a dark wooden surround, about two inches wide by three inches high, mounted securely but in a not-too-obvious place in a public and accessible space. The design on the medallion is shown in Figure 11.3.

No further clues: that's it. So put what you've learnt into practice. Prove that you can dowse: find it.

It may sound a daunting task at first, but it's actually little different from searching for a missing ring or a missing person, which some professional dowsers do on a regular basis. And we have covered every aspect of how to do this in the exercises in this book. The rest of it is dealing with Reality Department: creating the confidence and discipline to get something to work in the real world.

There are no tricks. It's just a straightforward dowsing task. There is only one target medallion in each area: so when you scan the map with your preferred map dowsing technique, you'll know you've got something wrong somewhere if more than one place is indicated. You'll also know that something's wrong if *no* place is indicated. (This assumes that someone hasn't moved the target: but that's a risk we'll have to take.)

All you have to do is use a standard set of dowsing techniques, first

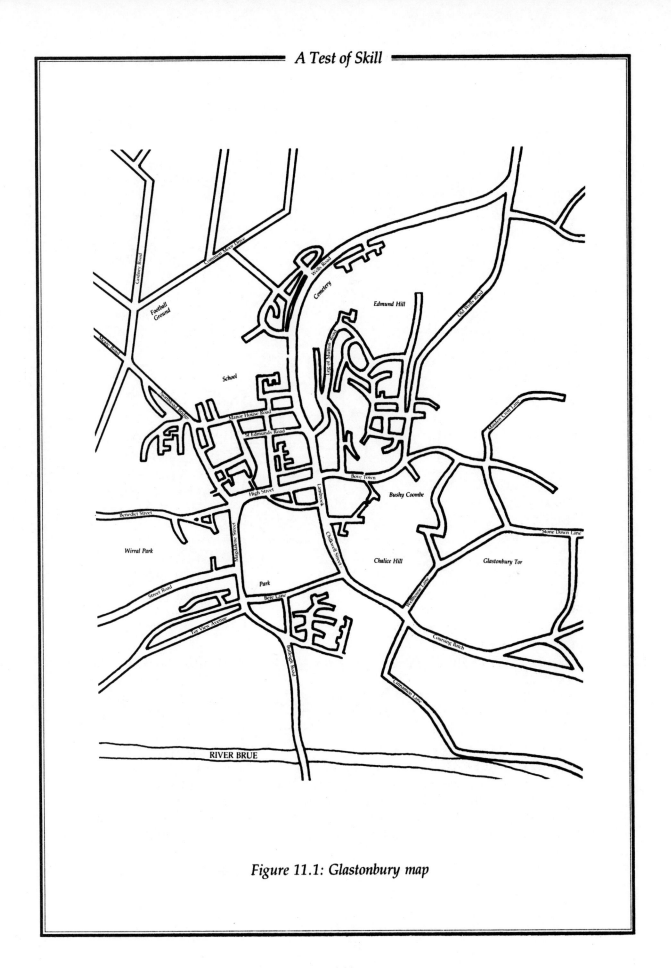

Figure 11.1: Glastonbury map

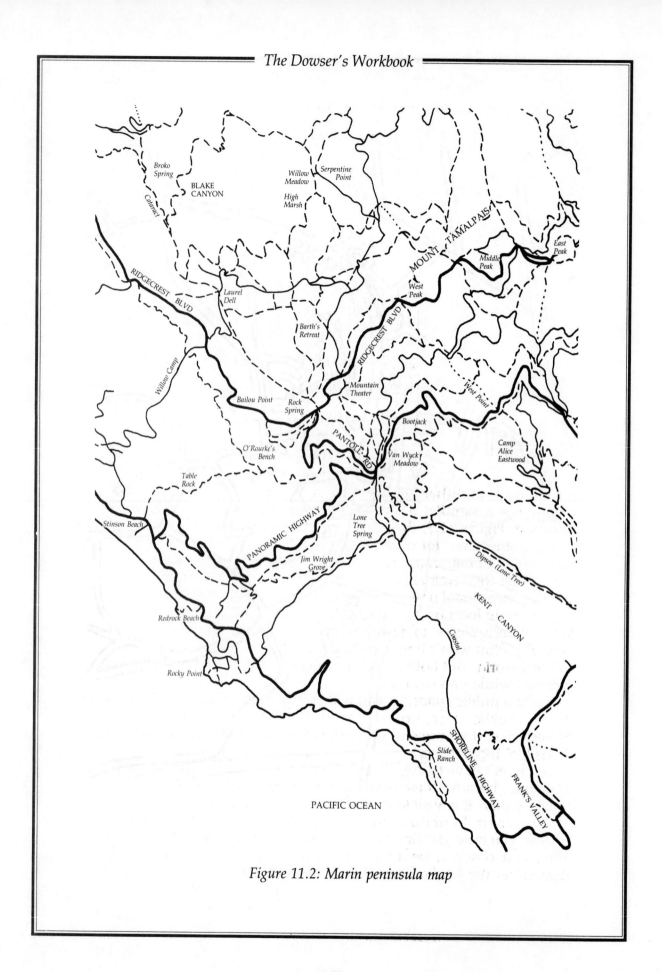

Figure 11.2: Marin peninsula map

Figure 11.3: The target medallion

on the map, and then on the ground, to find the exact location of the target. For a sample, it's probably easiest to use a photocopy of the design in Figure 11.3; though bear in mind that you're looking for the target, rather than for other copies of this book! Or, if you prefer, you can obtain a brass copy of the actual medallion from the craftspeople who made the original target: the details are in the Appendix.

Use a directional or coordinate technique on the map to work out the approximate location of the target; then go there, and apply the same kind of techniques to find its precise position. Then start looking, carefully. You won't find it unless you *do* go out into the field, out into the real world. But both places are in great areas for a holiday: so enjoy yourself while you're at it!

It is in a public space, so you will be able to get at it. Equally, because it's in a public space, do treat the area with respect. You don't have to be secretive; if you're shy about dowsing in public, just use one of the 'invisible' techniques.

You won't have to dig, or use dowsing techniques to find its depth or whatever, because it isn't buried; and a metal detector won't help you much, either. It is visible, though you'll have to know where to look in order to see it. Your dowsing tools should be able to lead you there; but equally you may just find yourself looking at it, without quite knowing how. Just observe, be aware, let your wider senses take you there. Remember the Fool's Law, that 'things can go right if you let them—

especially if you let them go right in unexpected ways'. As we've seen, almost anything could be considered dowsing, since it's all co-incidence in the end: perhaps the only real form of cheating would be to ask someone else where they found it. Assuming that that isn't the case, then, you'll still need some good overall awareness of one kind or another if you're going to find it, whichever way you do it. That's the test.

(When you find the target of this exercise, please *do not* remove it: leave it there so that other readers can test *their* skills, for as long as possible. As an added caution, in case you might think about removing it, remember that you could find some confused dowsers knocking at your door if you do—so don't! In case someone does remove either of the targets, though, the respective Society of Dowsers in each country has photographs and other details of their siting.)

Oh, and there is a prize: a silver copy of the target medallion, mounted as a pendant, for the first six claimants—three for each of the two sites—providing some kind of proof, such as a photograph. And no, a map-dowsing guess is *not* proof enough: you do have to prove that you've found it in the real world! You'll have to get a friend to check your results for you if you can't get there yourself. For continuity, the American Society of Dowsers has kindly agreed to act as a co-ordinator for the Californian target—their address is in the Appendix. (Note, though, that you must include a stamped self-addressed envelope with any enquiry, otherwise we won't be able to deal with it.)

So over to you: go to it!

An addendum

If that wasn't enough of a test to prove that you're a champion dowser, here's another, to test your wits and skills still further. I'd originally arranged with a friend, an active member of the San Francisco chapter of the American Society of Dowsers, to place the Californian target on some land where he has a cabin, up in the redwood forests of Mendocino County. But we thought about it for a while, and realized that it is rather a long way from anywhere, and it's also anything but public: there's a locked gate in the way, and some very privacy-conscious neighbours. So that was the end of that idea.

Well, not quite. Alex still wanted to join in the fun: so we revised our plans a little. We've placed two more copies of the target medallion for you to look for, one outside his home, the other close to his cabin in Mendocino.

His home is on the east side of San Francisco Bay (the opposite side from Marin, where the main target is located); his cabin is near Philo. But where are they exactly?

That's the test. Find them.

Figure 11.4: The classical labyrinth pattern

A couple of additional clues. Alex is keen on mazes and labyrinths, and the target in each case is close to one: a turf maze in his front garden at home, and a large classical labyrinth in Mendocino. (Now you know what to look for if you go to the extent of renting a plane!) And you *could* cheat by looking up Alex's number in the phone directory: his surname is in this section somewhere... for which you could dowse, of course.

More questions: the Mendocino target is mounted on a large, odd-shaped building that's not a house: what is it? What is its shape? What colour is it? And what diameter is the labyrinth?

The prize? You get to meet Alex and others of the San Francisco dowsers, and talk with them about dowsing and labyrinths!

And whatever you do with your dowsing, have fun!

Appendices

A: Further reading

You can't learn everything about dowsing just from this one book, of course. So here are some suggestions for further reading on dowsing and related subjects:

General dowsing

Christopher Bird, *The Divining Hand* (E.P. Dutton, New York, 1979). Well researched, with a lot of interesting descriptions and a large bibliography: a large-format 'coffee-table' book on dowsing.

Tom Graves, *The Diviner's Handbook* (The Aquarian Press, Wellingborough, England, 1986). Originally published in 1976 as *Dowsing: Techniques and Applications*, it's the companion volume to this book, and looks at dowsing from a more descriptive point of view.

D. Jurriaanse, *The Practical Pendulum Book* (Samuel Weiser Inc, New York, 1986). A small introductory volume with a comprehensive set of charts for use with the pendulum. Also available from the Aquarian Press, Wellingborough, England, complete with ready-made pendulum.

Tom Lethbridge, *Ghost and Divining Rod* (Routledge and Kegan Paul, London, England, 1963). A representative title from the nine books Lethbridge wrote on dowsing and related subjects: well worth reading not just for the description of the 'long pendulum' system, but also for his delightful writing style.

Sig Lonegren, *Spiritual Dowsing* (Gothic Image, Glastonbury, England, 1986). A good book with an American viewpoint—Sig is a former Trustee of the American Society of Dowsers—it has a useful emphasis on psychological and personal-growth aspects of dowsing.

Maj. Gen. James Scott-Elliott, *Dowsing—One Man's Way* (Neville Spearman, Jersey, 1977). Written by a former President of the British Society of Dowsers, it's exactly what the title says: a clear, no-frills description, with some very good case studies, of one man's way of dowsing.

Dowsing and healing

Elizabeth Baerlein and Lavender Dower, *Healing with Radionics* (Thorsons, Wellingborough, England, 1980). A general introduction to the principles and practice of using radionic instruments, as an extension of dowsing, to assist in the healing process.

David Tansley, *Radionics and the Subtle Anatomy of Man* (Health Science Press, England, 1974). One of a number of useful books written by this leading theorist and practitioner of radionics and medical dowsing.

Vernon D. Wethered, *An Introduction to Medical Radiaesthesia and Radionics* (C.W. Daniel, London, 1957). A slightly dated but still useful summary of medical aspects of dowsing.

Other aspects of dowsing and related subjects

Tom Graves, *Needles of Stone Revisited* (Gothic Image, Glastonbury, England, 1986). A comprehensive survey of the 'earth energies' field and its implications, using dowsing surveys of patterns both below and above ground as its starting-point, but also covering geomancy, ghost-hunting, parapsychology, pagan views of reality, and much more besides.

Francis Hitching, *Pendulum: The Psi Connection* (Fontana, London, 1977). A journalist's view of dowsing: history, interviews, case studies and some interesting pieces of practical research.

J.C. Maby and T. Bedford Franklin, *The Physics of the Divining Rod* (Bell, London, 1939). The results of a research project commissioned by the British Society of Dowsers, this is one of the few systematic scientific studies of dowsing ever published. (Out of print, but the British Society of Dowsers has copies in its library.)

Guy Underwood, *The Pattern of the Past* (Abacus, London, England, 1974). Now a classic, this is a fascinating—if at times idiosyncratic—study of dowsable patterns at a wide variety of sacred and not-so-sacred sites.

B: Contacts

You can only learn so much from books and from working on your own: at some point you really will need others with whom to work and experiment. Working with others, helping each other in testing the reliability of your work, you'll discover far more than you can on your own.

Good bookshops and magazines will be able to advise you of likely contacts in your area, or of suitable events to go and see—or more to the point, to join in. But perhaps the most important source of information and contacts will be the national dowsers' societies: working with other members, whether experienced or relative new-comers, you're likely to learn most of all.

The *British Society of Dowsers* is the oldest, founded in 1933, with members actively involved in every aspect of practical dowsing. One of its great strengths is that it concentrates on practicalities rather than trying to find out 'how it *really* works'. The most popular interest is probably the use of dowsing in health and healing, although you'll find members applying their dowsing to anything from 'conventional' water divining and civil engineering to archaeology and everything beyond. The society publishes a quarterly journal, and each year organizes several lecture meetings in London and an annual conference (at a different location each year). Dowsers in Scotland have their own national organization, the *Scottish Dowsers*, which is affiliated to the British Society. Both organisations also have a number of local groups in various parts of the country, most of which run their own lecture schedule and, in some cases, training courses. To get in touch with these groups, contact Michael Rust, the current Secretary of the British Society of Dowsers, at Sycamore Cottage, Tamley Lane, Hastingleigh, Ashford, Kent TN25 5HW.

The *American Society of Dowsers* is a large, active body with many local chapters scattered throughout the United States. The Society's base is in Danville, Vermont (Dowsers' Hall, Danville, VT 05828-0024). Several hundred members and non-members attend the week-long annual convention there in September each year, with a dowsing school and dozens of workshops and seminars for the attendees. (The convention all but takes over the small town: workshops are held not just in the town hall, but the church, the school, the fire station and practically everywhere else as well!) For obvious reasons, water diviners are more common in the American Society than the British, but once again almost every aspect of dowsing is represented. Reflecting the realities of scale and distance in the States, the local chapters are larger and more autonomous than their British equivalents: some chapters or groups of chapters even put on their own conventions—the 'Mile High' dowsers' group in Denver, Colorado, for example, or the West Coast convention in Santa Cruz in July each year.

C: Sample for 'A real test of skill'

The brass target medallions for the 'A real test of skill' exercise were made by Gino and Judith Schiavone from my original design, derived from a woodcut in Agricola's *De Re Metallica*. Copies of the medallion, for use as a sample or 'witness' for that exercise, are available from them. These copies are acid-etched on a brass tablet, at 40 per cent of the size of the original: provisional price at the time of writing is $10.00 (plus mail, and sales tax where applicable). For further details, contact them direct at 'In Her Image', PO Box 353, Pt Reyes Station, CA 94956, USA.